Sounds Abound

Listening, Rhyming, and Reading

by Hugh Catts, Ph.D. & Tina Williamson

Skill	Ages	Grades
■ phonological awareness	■ 4 through 7	■ PreK through 2

Evidence-Based Practice

- ASHA (2001) states that speech-language pathologists play an integral role in identifying children who are at risk of developing reading disorders and providing intervention on oral speech and language skills, including phonological awareness skills. Direct intervention in the preschool years may reduce later reading and spelling difficulties.

- Training in phonological awareness is critical to reading success, and manipulating phonemes in words is highly effective across all literary domains and outcomes (NRP, 2000).

- Tasks that require students to manipulate spoken units larger than phonemes are simpler for beginners than tasks requiring phoneme manipulation. Instruction often begins by teaching children to manipulate larger units and includes such activities as rhyming, breaking sentences into words, and breaking words into syllables (NRP, 2000).

- Blending and segmenting skills must be present in order to decode unfamiliar words. Thus, in order to improve decoding, a student must have a foundation of these skills (Schuele & Boudreau, 2008).

- Explicit instruction in phonemic awareness and phonetic decoding skills produces stronger reading growth in children with phonological weaknesses than do approaches that do not teach these skills explicitly (Torgesen, 2000).

Sounds Abound Listening, Rhyming, and Reading incorporates these principles and is also based on expert professional practice.

References

American Speech-Language-Hearing Association (ASHA). (2001). *Roles and responsibilities of speech-language pathologists with respect to reading and writing in children and adolescents* [Position Statement]. Retrieved January 21, 2010, from www.asha.org/docs/pdf/PS2001-00104.pdf

National Reading Panel (NRP). (2000). *Teaching children to read: An evidence based assessment of the scientific research literature on reading and its implication for reading instruction – Reports of the subgroups.* Retrieved January 21, 2010, from www.nichd.nih.gov/publications/nrp/upload/report.pdf

Schuele, C.M., & Boudreau, D. (2008). Phonological awareness intervention: Beyond the basics. *Language, Speech, and Hearing Services in Schools, 39*, 3-20.

Torgesen, J.K. (2000). Individual differences in response to early interventions in reading: The lingering problem of treatment resisters. *Learning Disabilities Research & Practice, 15*, 55-64.

LinguiSystems

LinguiSystems, Inc.
3100 4th Avenue
East Moline, IL 61244
800-776-4332
FAX: 800-577-4555
Email: service@linguisystems.com
Web: linguisystems.com

Copyright © 1993 LinguiSystems, Inc.

All of our products are copyrighted to protect the fine work of our authors. You may copy the worksheets only as needed for your own use with students. Any other reproduction or distribution of the pages in this book is prohibited, including copying the entire book to use as another primary source or "master" copy.

Printed in the U.S.A.

ISBN 10: 1-55999-394-4
ISBN 13: 978-1-55999-394-4

About The Authors

Hugh W. Catts, Ph.D, CCC-SP, is an Associate Professor in the Department of Speech-Language-Hearing at the University of Kansas. He teaches courses in communicative disorders and language learning disabilities. His research and clinical interests concern the relationship between oral and written language disorders. He is currently involved in the early identification and remediation of language-based reading disabilities.

Hugh W. Catts

Tina Olsen, M.A., CCC, is a speech-language pathologist working in the public school system. Since graduating from Augustana College, she received her master's degree from the University of Kansas and presently works with children ages birth to five in Kansas City, Kansas. She has a particular interest in the relationship between reading and the development of language.

August 1993

Tina Olsen

Acknowledgement

The authors would like to thank Melissa Thomas for her valuable assistance in the preparation of these materials.

May all children experience the joy of reading.
-Hugh and Tina

"For you and your students -
The best language, learning, and thinking materials.
LinguiSystems' promise to you."

We welcome your comments on
Sounds Abound and other LinguiSystems products.

Illustrator: Tony Vandercar

Table of Contents

Scope and Sequence 4

Introduction 5
    Overview of *Sounds Abound*
    What is Phonological Awareness?
    How is Spoken Language Related to Reading?
    How is Phonological Awareness Related to Reading?

Sound Awareness Books 9
    References for:
    Nursery Rhyme Books
    Picture Books
    Poetry Books
    Song Books
    Fingerplay and Rhyme Books

Rhyme 13
    Rhyme Judgment 14
    Rhyme Production 43
    Rhyme Play 61
    Rhyme Pretest 70
    Rhyme Posttest 71

Beginnings and Endings 72
    Sound Judgment 73
    Sound Production 106
    Sound Play 122
    Beginnings and Endings Pretest 127
    Beginnings and Endings Posttest 128

Segmenting and Blending 129
    Segmenting Syllables 130
    Blending Syllables 146
    Segmenting Phonemes 153
    Blending Phonemes 165
    Syllable/Phoneme Segmentation Pretest 175
    Syllable/Phoneme Segmentation Posttest 176
    Syllable/Phoneme Blending Pretest 177
    Syllable/Phoneme Blending Posttest 178

Putting Sounds Together with Letters 179

References 188

Scope and Sequence

Sound Awareness Books

Suggested materials to introduce children to the sounds of language

Rhyme

Rhyme Judgment: activities to teach children to make judgments about rhymes

Rhyme Production: activities to teach children to provide rhyming words

Rhyme Play: songs and games to teach children to produce rhymes

Beginnings and Endings

Sound Judgment: activities to teach children to make judgments about the speech sounds at the beginning and end of words

Sound Production: activities to teach children to produce words that begin with the same sound as target words

Sound Play: songs and games to teach children to produce words that begin with the same sound as target words

Segmenting and Blending

Segmenting Syllables: activities to teach children to segment the syllables in words

Blending Syllables: activities to teach children to blend syllables into words

Segmenting Phonemes: activities to teach children to segment the phonemes in words

Blending Phonemes: activities to teach children to blend phonemes into words

Putting Sounds Together with Letters

Letters and Sounds: activities to teach children to use letters to make words; children will learn that letters represent phonemes

Evaluation

Evaluation: A Pretest and a Posttest are provided at the end of several sections to informally evaluate children's skills in a particular area.

Introduction

The alphabet is a wondrous invention, perhaps the greatest of all times. This writing system allows one who is fluent in spoken language to quickly become fluent in written language. By representing the speech sounds in spoken words, the alphabet enables the reader to translate printed words into their spoken equivalents. Spoken equivalents can then be recognized in much the same way that speech is recognized.

Using an alphabet is different from understanding and producing speech in at least one important way. This difference concerns how aware one needs to be of the sounds of language. Spoken language does not require a conscious awareness of the speech sounds in words. Speech is produced and understood automatically, with little conscious attention given to speech sounds. An alphabetic language, on the other hand, requires explicit speech sound awareness. Because the alphabet represents speech sounds, the beginning reader must become aware of these sounds in order to understand how the alphabet works.

Awareness of speech sounds is not always easy for young children. There is considerable variability between young children in their speech sound awareness. This variability appears to be a major determinant of how quickly and easily children learn to read an alphabetic language.

Sounds Abound is designed to help young children become aware of the speech sounds in words and how the alphabet represents these sounds.

Overview of *Sounds Abound*

Sounds Abound is divided into five sections:

• *Speech Sound Awareness* is a list of references that offer practice in sound repetition and sound play. These materials can be used with young children or those with very limited phonological awareness as an introduction to the sounds of language.

• *Rhyme* more explicitly draws children's attention to the sounds of rhyming words. Materials in this section require children to make judgments about rhymes and produce rhyming words. Rhyming games and songs are included to help children become aware of rhyme in a fun, interactive way.

• *Beginning and Ending Sounds* draws children's attention to the beginning and ending sounds of words. Activities require children to make judgments about the sounds in words and to produce words with the same beginning sounds. Sound games and songs are also included to help children learn about the sounds in words.

- *Segmenting and Blending* teaches children to segment and blend the sounds in words. Segmentation and blending are introduced first for syllables and then for phonemes.

- *Putting Sounds Together with Words* introduces an abbreviated alphabet to teach children how letters are used to represent the sounds of words.

Pretests and Posttests are included for several of the sections of this book to help determine children's speech sound awareness.

Not all children will need to start at the beginning of this program or complete all of the activities at each level. Some children may only require limited exposure to these materials in order to gain the necessary speech sound awareness to read an alphabetic language. On the other hand, some children will need much repetition of these materials in order to acquire speech sound awareness.

This program is intended to be used as a supplement to more comprehensive reading programs. Although speech sound awareness is the key to understanding the alphabet, there is much more to skilled reading than alphabetic knowledge. Skilled readers can use the alphabet to recognize words, but more importantly, they understand the meaning of what they read. Therefore, reading instruction must also provide children with the skills and opportunities to learn to comprehend what they read.

What is Phonological Awareness?

Speech sound awareness, or phonological awareness, is the conscious awareness of the sounds of language. It is the ability to reflect on the sounds in words separate from the meanings of words. Phonological awareness includes:

- the awareness of the suprasegmental aspects of speech, such as phonological length, voice quality, and intonation.

- the awareness of the segmental properties of speech, such as the appreciation that words may rhyme or begin/end with the same sound segment.

- more analytical knowledge which allows one to divide words into syllables or phonemes and to count, add, or delete these sound segments.

Early in life, young children show little awareness of the sounds in words. Their attention is focused on the meaning of words. The sounds that make up words go unnoticed. However, during the preschool years, most children begin to show interest in the sounds of words. Preschool children may comment on the fact that a word sounds odd, that it rhymes, or that it begins with the same sound as another word. Preschool children also frequently engage in sound play activities in which they create rhyming or alliterative sequences.

The development of phonological awareness appears to be related to both early literacy experiences and cognitive-linguistic development. Research suggests that early experience with nursery rhymes and other literacy materials may foster children's awareness of the sounds of language. For example, researchers have shown that children's knowledge of nursery rhymes at age three is related to their sensitivity to rhyme and phonemes at ages four to six.

In addition to literacy experience, phonological awareness appears to develop with maturation of a specific cognitive-linguistic ability. This emerging ability, which is independent of general intelligence, allows children to more fully reflect on the sounds in words.

How is Spoken Language Related to Reading?

Reading is a language-based activity. Beginning readers can use the language knowledge they have acquired through speaking and listening. This knowledge plays an important role in understanding written language. Children's vocabulary and knowledge of sentence and discourse structures is essential for comprehending what they read.

Comprehension of written materials is the primary goal of most reading, but a major task facing beginning readers is learning how to recognize written words. Beginning readers can use their knowledge of spoken language to help in written word recognition. Semantic and syntactic knowledge can provide the contextual support that may allow children to predict and identify some unfamiliar words.

In an alphabetic language, there's an even richer source of spoken language knowledge that can be used for the purpose of word recognition. An alphabetic language uses a symbol system that represents the sounds of words. By converting a sequence of letters into a spoken form, the reader can recognize unfamiliar written words on the basis of a previously acquired spoken vocabulary.

How is Phonological Awareness Related to Reading?

Beginning readers must gain a conscious awareness of the phonemes in words to learn to use an alphabetic language. This awareness of phonemes generally does not come naturally with spoken language development. In spoken language, speech sounds are produced and understood automatically, below the level of conscious awareness. Most preschool and kindergarten children lack an awareness of the individual phonemes in words. These children do not realize that words can be divided into phonemes. However, many children can divide words into syllables and have an appreciation of the fact that words may rhyme or have similar beginnings and endings.

Developing a conscious awareness of phonemes generally requires some explicit instruction. For most children, this comes in first grade when they learn the alphabet and how it works. Children learn how to divide words into phonemes and represent these phonemes with letters. This sound-symbol correspondence serves as the basis for learning to read an alphabetic language.

Research indicates that how quickly children become proficient in using the alphabet to read is related to their phonological awareness. Studies have consistently found differences in phonological awareness between good and poor readers. Children who enter first grade with some awareness of the sounds of language and who quickly learn that words can be divided into phonemes generally become the better readers in the early grades. On the other hand, children who begin school with a limited appreciation of rhyme and alliteration and who struggle with learning to segment phonemes, may become poor readers.

Research has also shown that differences in phonological awareness can be measured before children begin school and that these differences are predictive of reading success in school. For example, studies have shown that measures of rhyme detection and syllable segmentation in kindergarten are among the best predictors of reading in the early school grades.

Phonological awareness appears to be particularly difficult for children with reading disabilities. These children often have very little awareness of speech sounds and experience great difficulties learning to segment words into phonemes. These problems have led researchers to conclude that deficits in phonological awareness may be a primary cause of many early reading disabilities.

Recent studies have shown that readers who have problems acquiring phonological awareness can benefit from systematic training in phonological awareness. Studies have shown that these children can be taught to become more aware of speech sounds and that this awareness can have a direct effect on their early reading achievement. *Sounds Abound* is an outgrowth of this research. Many of the techniques employed in these training studies have been incorporated into *Sounds Abound*.

Hugh
Tina

Sound Awareness Books

In this section, lists of children's books involving rhyme and alliteration are presented. Also included are lists of books containing poems, songs, and fingerplays. Use these materials to introduce children to the sounds of language.

By interacting with these materials, children can gain an initial appreciation of the sounds of language. To begin, have the children listen to the stories, poems, fingerplays, or songs. After some repetition, have the children actively participate in these activities.

These materials can also be used in many creative ways to promote speech sound awareness. For example, children can be encouraged to create new verses to rhymes and songs or to alter rhymes or poems by inserting new words and phrases.

Nursery Rhyme Books

A Treasury of Mother Goose. (1984). New York: Simon Schuster.

Aylesworth, J. (1992). *The Cat and the Fiddle and More.* New York: Maxwell Macmillan International.

de Angeli, M. (1953). *Book of Nursery and Mother Goose Rhymes.* New York: Doubleday.

de Paola, T. (1985). *Mother Goose.* New York: G. P. Putnam's Sons.

Langley, J. (1990). *Rain, Rain, Go Away Book of Nursery Rhymes.* New York: DIAL Books.

The Real Mother Goose. (1916). New York: Checkerboard Press.

Schwartz, A. (1989). *I Saw You in the Bathtub and Other Folk Rhymes.* New York: Harper Collins Publishers.

Sutherland, Z. (1991). *The Orchard Book of Nursery Rhymes.* New York: Orchard Books.

Wilkes, A. (1992). *Animal Nursery Rhymes.* New York: Dorling Kindersley.

Sound Awareness Books, continued

Picture Books

Ahlberg, J., and Ahlberg, A. (1978). *Each Peach Pear Plum.* New York: Random House.

Base, G. *Animalia.* (1986). New York: Abrams.

Berenstain, S., and Berenstain, J. (1980). *The Berenstain Bears' Christmas Tree.* New York: Random House.

Bernard-Westcott, N. (1980). *I Know an Old Lady Who Swallowed a Fly.* Boston: Little, Brown, and Co.

Brandreth, G. (1978). *The Biggest Tongue Twister Book in the World.* New York: Sterling Publishing Co.

Brown, M. (1987). *Play Rhymes.* New York: E. P. Dutton.

Chute, M. (1974). *Rhymes About Us.* New York: Dutton and Company, Inc.

Eastman, P. (1974). *The Alphabet Book.* New York: Random House.

Gackenback, D. (1986). *Timid Timothy's Tongue Twisters.* New York: Holiday House.

Le Seig, T. (1989). *The Pop-Up Mice of Mr. Brice.* New York: Random House.

Martin, B. Jr., and Carle, E. (1991). *Polar Bear, Polar Bear, What Do You Hear?* New York: Henry Holt and Company.

Moncure, J. (1984). *Word Bird Makes Words With Cat.* Mankato, MN: Child's World.

Schenk De Regniers, B. (1972). *It Does Not Say Meow and Other Animal Riddle Rhymes.* New York: Clarion Books.

Schwartz, A. (1982). *Busy Buzzing Bumblebee and Other Tongue Twisters.* New York: Harper & Row.

Seuss, Dr. (1963). *Hop on Pop.* New York: Random House.

Taylor, J. (1992). *Twinkle, Twinkle, Little Star.* New York: Books of Wonder.

This Old Man. (1974). New York: Grosset & Dunlap.

Sound Awareness Books, continued

Thaler, M. (1988). *In the Middle of a Puddle.* New York: Harper Collins Children's Books.

Thomas, P. (1979). *There Are Rocks in My Socks Said the Ox to the Fox.* New York: Lathrop, Lee, and Shepard Co.

Poetry Books

Amery, H. (1992). *The Usborne Book of Children's Poems.* London: Usborne Publishing Ltd.

Carrol, L. (1987). *Jabberwocky.* New York: Harry N. Abrams Inc. Publishers.

Clifton, L. (1974). *Everett Anderson's Year.* New York: Holt, Rinehart & Winston.

Cole, J. (1984). *A New Treasury of Children's Poetry: Old Favorites and New Discoveries.* New York: Doubleday.

Cole, J. (1989). *Anna Banana 101 Jump-Rope Rhymes.* New York: William Morrow & Company, Inc.

de Paola, T. (1988). *Book of Poems.* New York: G. P. Putnam's Sons.

Dunn, S., and Parmenter, L. (1987). *Butterscotch Dreams.* New Hampshire: Heinemann Educational Books, Inc.

Ferris, H. (1957). *Favorite Poems Old and New.* New York: Delacorte Press.

Johnston, T. (1990). *I'm Gonna Tell Mama I Want an Iguana.* New York: G. P. Putnam's Sons.

My First Book of Poems. (1989). Nashville: Ideals Children's Books.

The Nonsense Poems of Edward Lear. (1991). New York: Clarion Books.

Prelutsky, J. (1986). *Read-Aloud Rhymes for the Very Young.* New York: Alfred A. Knopf.

Silverstein, S. (1981). *A Light in the Attic.* New York: Golden Press.

Werner, J. (1947). *The Big Golden Book of Poetry: 85 Children's Favorites.* New York: Golden Press.

Sound Awareness Books, continued

Song Books

ACHIEV Red Language Sing-A-Longs. (1990). East Moline, IL: LinguiSystems, Inc.

Amery, H. (1988). *The Usborne Children's Songbook*. London: Usborne Publishing Ltd.

Emerson, S., and Frank, M. (1992). *Nursery Rhyme Songbook*. New York: Kingfisher Books.

Fox, D. (1987). *Go In and Out the Window: An Illustrated Songbook for Young People*. New York: Metropolitan Museum of Art.

Hart, J. (1989). *Singing Bee: A Collection of Children's Songs*. New York: William Morrow & Co.

McPhail, D. (1990). *The Mother Goose Songbook: 44 Favorite Rhymes with Music for Piano*. New York: Doubleday.

The Raffi Singable Songbook. (1980). New York: Crown Publishers, Inc.

Sing Hey Diddle Diddle: 66 Nursery Rhymes with Their Traditional Tunes. (1983). London: A & C Black.

Wood, J. (1990). *First Songs and Action Rhymes*. New York: Aladdin Books.

Yolen, J. (1992). *Mother Goose Songbook*. Homesdale: Boyds Mill Press.

Fingerplay and Rhyme Books

Brown, M. (1985). *Hand Rhymes*. New York: E. P. Dutton.

Brown, M. (1980). *Finger Rhymes*. New York: E. P. Dutton.

Elkins, S., and Kennedy, P. (1990). *Nursery Songs and Lap Games*. Nashville: Ideals Children's Books.

Glazer, T. (1973). *Eye Winker, Tom Tinker, Chin Chopper: Fifty Musical Fingerplays*. New York: Doubleday & Company, Inc.

Montgomerie, N. (1966). *This Little Pig Went to Market*. New York: Watts, Inc.

Wirth, M.; Stassevitch, V.; Shotwell, R.; and Stemmler, P. (1983). *Musical Games, Fingerplays, and Rhythmic Activities for Early Childhood*. West Nyack, NY: Parker Publishing Co., Inc.

Rhyme

Rhyme is a prominent feature of speech. Rhyme is found in poetry, songs, and many children's books and games. Young children enjoy nursery rhymes and rhyme games.

Rhyme is also a way of categorizing the words young children hear. Words like *cat*, *hat*, and *sat* can be grouped together by children on the basis of their common sound pattern. Because words in these categories often have similar spellings, children may use these rhyme categories when learning to read and spell.

This section on rhyme includes fun activities to help children appreciate and produce rhyming words. It's divided into the following three parts: rhyme judgment, rhyme production, and rhyme play.

In the rhyme judgment activities, children are asked to make judgments about whether or not words rhyme.

In the rhyme production activities, children are asked to say words that rhyme with the target words.

In the rhyme play activities, children will play games and sing songs to practice saying words that rhyme.

Activities with pictures are used initially in both the rhyme judgment and rhyme production activities. These activities are followed by word lists to be read aloud to children.

Rhyming Pairs?

Rhyme Judgment

Here is a list of words to refer to when completing the activities on pages 15-19.

Rhyming Pairs? 1, page 15

1. pan   fan
2. ice   dice
3. king   bed
4. moon   spoon
5. can   rake

Rhyming Pairs? 2, page 16

1. door   snow
2. house   mouse
3. box   three
4. plate   skate
5. bees   cheese

Rhyming Pairs? 3, page 17

1. goat   can
2. nut   cut
3. sock   pail
4. bee   knee
5. sink   wink

Rhyming Pairs? 4, page 18

1. flag   hat
2. sail   tail
3. mop   sheep
4. star   jar
5. snake   rake

Rhyming Pairs? 5, page 19

1. jail   duck
2. toe   bow
3. one   rain
4. frog   dog
5. egg   leg

Sounds Abound

Rhyming Pairs? 1   Name _____

Name the pictures in each row. If the words rhyme, draw circles around each picture.

1.		
2.		
3.		
4.		
5.		

Sounds Abound   15   Copyright © 1993 LinguiSystems, Inc.

Rhyming Pairs? 2

Name _____

Name the pictures in each row. If the words rhyme, draw an X on each picture.

1.		
2.		
3.		
4.		
5.		

Sounds Abound   16   Copyright © 1993 LinguiSystems, Inc.

Rhyming Pairs? 3

Name _____

Name the pictures in each row. If the words rhyme, draw a line through each of the pictures.

1.	goat	soup
2.	peanut	scissors
3.	sock	bucket
4.	fly	elbow
5.	sink	wink

Sounds Abound

Copyright © 1993 LinguiSystems, Inc.

Rhyming Pairs? 4   Name _____

Name the pictures in each row. If the words rhyme, say yes.

1.	flag	hat
2.	sail	tail
3.	mop	sheep
4.	star	bandage
5.	snake	rake

Sounds Abound   18   Copyright © 1993 LinguiSystems, Inc.

Rhyming Pairs? 5   Name _____

Name the pictures in each row. If the words rhyme, clap your hands.

1.	jail	duck
2.	toe	bow
3.	one	rain
4.	frog	dog
5.	egg	leg

Sounds Abound   19   Copyright © 1993 LinguiSystems, Inc.

Rhyming Pairs? 6

Rhyme Judgment

Read each word pair aloud. Ask the child to tell you if the two words rhyme.

1.	shade	made		21.	hot	big
2.	end	ball		22.	chest	best
3.	five	dive		23.	weed	pear
4.	gum	some		24.	rocks	clocks
5.	tell	ghost		25.	boot	shoot
6.	send	lend		26.	tight	right
7.	shoe	hide		27.	jog	boot
8.	fort	wall		28.	fight	light
9.	drink	pink		29.	hop	shop
10.	box	line		30.	gas	clown
11.	down	brown		31.	cold	gold
12.	spot	not		32.	sit	kit
13.	win	new		33.	pill	hot
14.	nine	line		34.	met	wet
15.	six	fix		35.	skirt	hurt
16.	key	sky		36.	mouth	south
17.	mouse	house		37.	cat	dog
18.	fox	help		38.	eye	buy
19.	four	door		39.	hand	sand
20.	shirt	dirt		40.	fell	tall

Sounds Abound

Rhyming Pairs? 7

Rhyme Judgment

Read each word pair aloud. Ask the child to tell you if the two words rhyme.

1. kid   gift
2. skin   twin
3. fight   night
4. bake   late
5. me   see
6. own   grown
7. leg   desk
8. bride   wide
9. come   dime
10. sneeze   breeze
11. led   red
12. peek   week
13. five   give
14. back   sack
15. ant   send
16. nail   light
17. paint   hot
18. tea   sea
19. mail   sail
20. deer   pair
21. like   hike
22. talk   chalk
23. kind   went
24. die   fly
25. hair   bear
26. fast   most
27. big   dig
28. win   green
29. roar   more
30. blow   go
31. pour   fire
32. toy   joy
33. fall   girl
34. cook   look
35. lick   trick
36. tree   me
37. ran   ham
38. rug   tug
39. meal   full
40. clock   sock

Sounds Abound   Copyright © 1993 LinguiSystems, Inc.

Matching Rhymes

Rhyme Judgment

Here is a list of words to refer to when completing the activities on pages 24-28.

Matching Rhymes 1, page 24

1. bat   snow   rat
2. wheel   seal   cake
3. gate   corn   plate
4. can   man   sail
5. top   shell   mop

Matching Rhymes 2, page 25

1. rain   chain   box
2. lamp   stamp   bee
3. nail   sock   jail
4. clown   crown   top
5. tail   clock   whale

Matching Rhymes 3, page 26

1. horn   shoe   corn
2. sun   one   sled
3. deer   pool   ear
4. shoe   two   pig
5. fire   sock   tire

Matching Rhymes *continued*

Rhyme Judgment

Matching Rhymes 4, page 27

1. door   four   skate
2. ring   wing   ball
3. car   ear   star
4. truck   nut   duck
5. pie   eye   kite

Matching Rhymes 5, page 28

1. three   sheep   bee
2. boat   goat   rope
3. kite   hat   light
4. chair   car   bear
5. stick   brick   dog

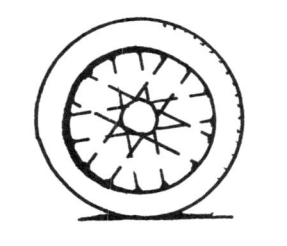

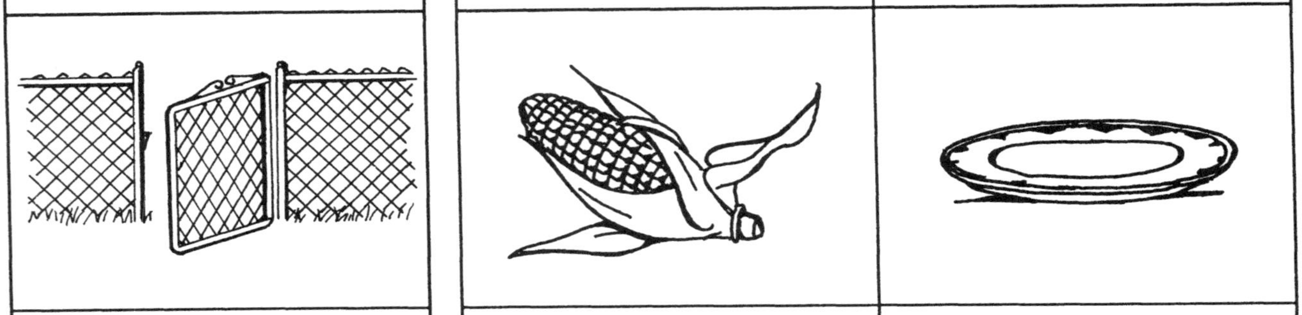

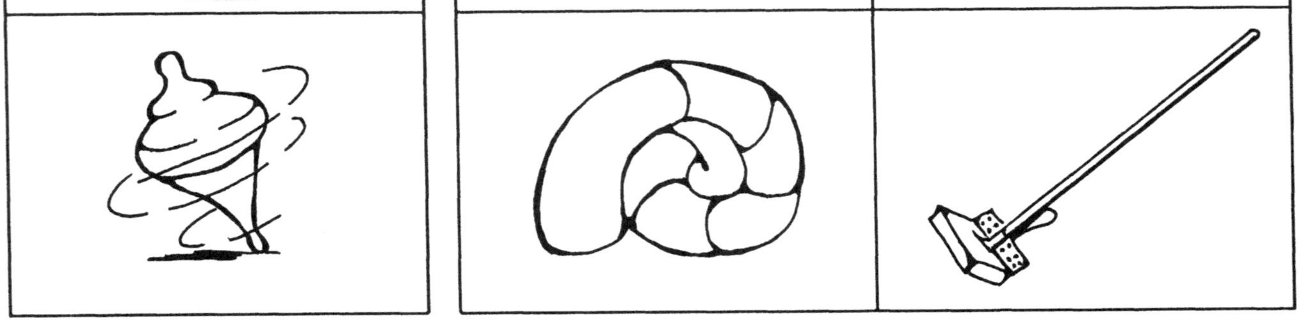

Matching Rhymes 1   Name _____

Color the picture in each row that rhymes with the first word.

1.	bat	house in snow	rat
2.	tire	seal	cake
3.	gate	corn	plate
4.	soup	old man	tent
5.	top	snail	broom

Sounds Abound   24   Copyright © 1993 LinguiSystems, Inc.

Matching Rhymes 2

Name _____

Put an X on the picture in each row that rhymes with the first word.

1.	rain	chain	box
2.	lamp	stamp	bee
3.	nail	sock	jail
4.	clown	crown	top
5.	tail	clock	whale

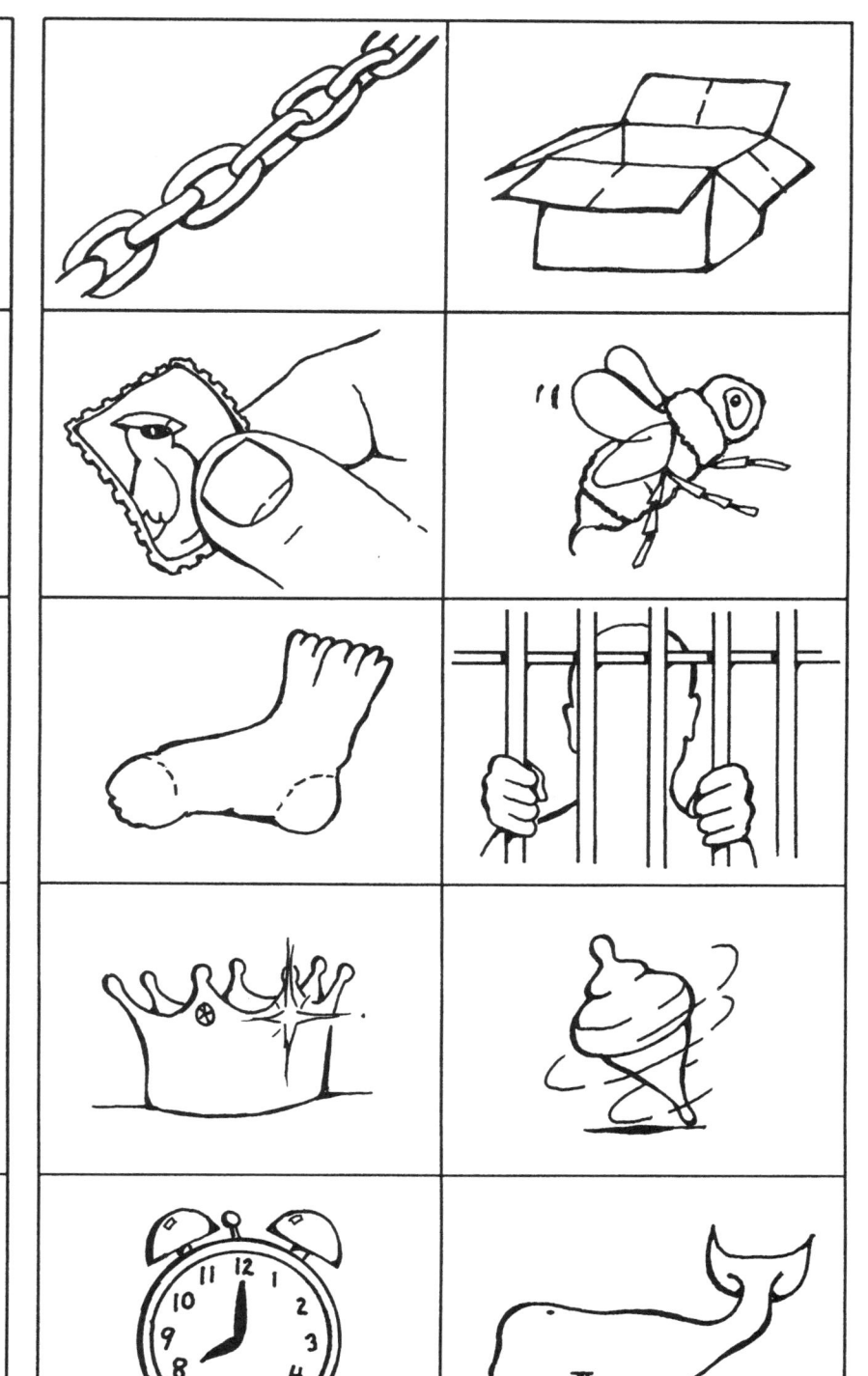

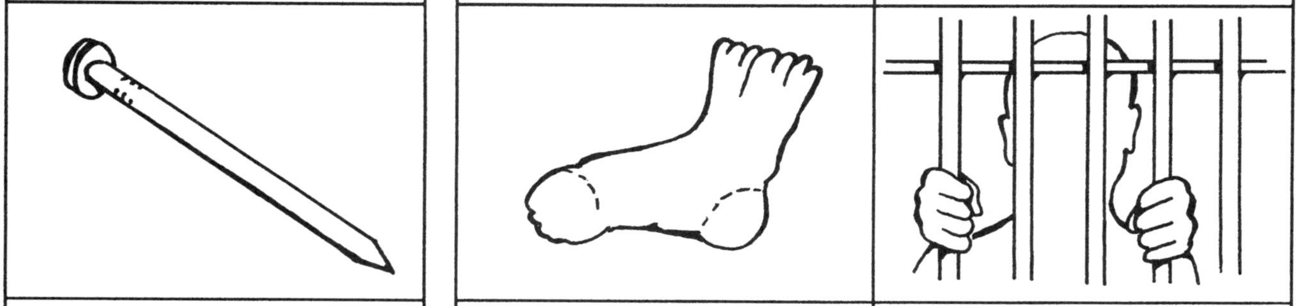

Sounds Abound   Copyright © 1993 LinguiSystems, Inc

Matching Rhymes 3

Name _____

Circle the picture in each row that rhymes with the first word.

1.
2.
3.
4.
5.

Sounds Abound 26 Copyright © 1993 LinguiSystems, Inc.

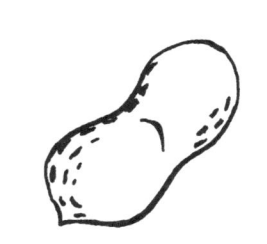

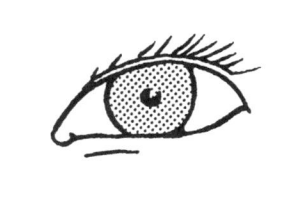

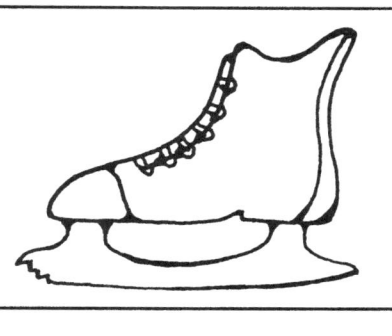

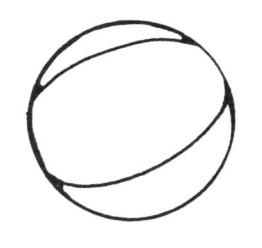

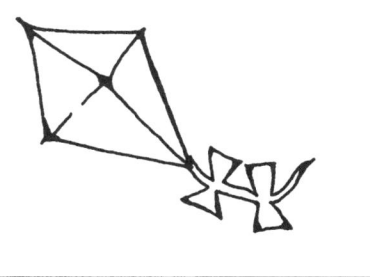

Matching Rhymes 4   Name _____

Put a line through the picture in each row that rhymes with the first word.

1. door | 4 | skate
2. ring | wing | ball
3. car | ear | star
4. truck | peanut | duck
5. pie | eye | kite

Sounds Abound   27   Copyright © 1993 LinguiSystems, Inc

Matching Rhymes 5   Name _____

Put an X on the picture in each row that rhymes with the first word.

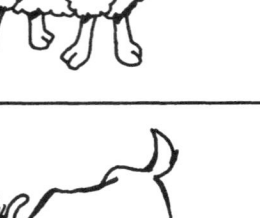

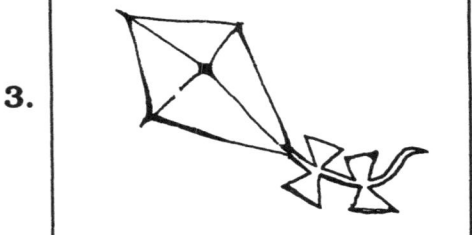

1.	3	sheep	bee
2.	boat	goat	snake
3.	kite	hat	light
4.	chair	car	bear
5.	stick	brick	dog

Sounds Abound   28   Copyright © 1993 LinguiSystems, Inc.

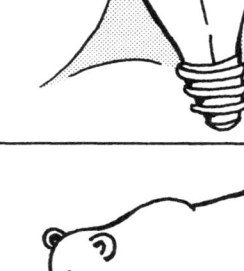

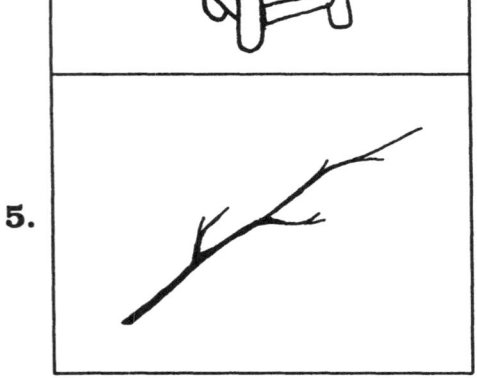

Matching Rhymes 6

Rhyme Judgment

Read each set of words aloud. Ask the child to tell you which word rhymes with the first word.

1. wrap   nap   toy
2. beat   gum   sheet
3. mat   cook   fat
4. meal   peel   talk
5. gave   tight   brave
6. need   read   blow
7. roll   goal   peek
8. fail   cold   pail
9. test   west   green
10. turn   dig   burn
11. head   dead   joy
12. hop   night   drop
13. round   hike   pound
14. bird   word   look
15. last   week   fast
16. red   hot   bed
17. torn   born   sand
18. feel   knife   meal
19. pear   tune   bear
20. spoon   moon   blue

Sounds Abound

Matching Rhymes 7

Rhyme Judgment

Read each set of words aloud. Ask the child to tell you which word rhymes with the first word.

1.	mouth	south	right
2.	rope	hope	see
3.	witch	sit	rich
4.	goose	loose	clock
5.	tape	grape	fix
6.	give	brown	live
7.	spell	fell	lead
8.	frame	blame	wire
9.	splash	nine	trash
10.	pay	clay	like
11.	cheer	bump	tear
12.	bubble	cookie	trouble
13.	sweat	bell	jet
14.	play	tray	snake
15.	dinner	honey	winner
16.	joke	poke	light
17.	money	hurry	funny
18.	bug	rug	bat
19.	father	bother	weather
20.	can	seem	man

Sounds Abound · Copyright © 1993 LinguiSystems, Inc.

Matching Rhymes 8

Rhyme Judgment

Read each set of words aloud. Ask the child to tell you which word rhymes with the first word.

1. thick — sick — bride
2. grow — rock — row
3. pack — crack — shade
4. bake — roar — take
5. cold — broke — sold
6. seven — heaven — drinking
7. found — cow — sound
8. pick — trick — give
9. letter — better — puppy
10. sleep — cheap — peek
11. jeans — wins — beans
12. nice — rose — slice
13. knock — sock — rob
14. sew — coat — show
15. Mike — light — bike
16. night — goat — sight
17. blue — two — roof
18. pen — hen — clean
19. hot — rot — flock
20. make — grape — take

Sounds Abound   31   Copyright © 1993 LinguiSystems, Inc.

Matching Rhymes 9

Rhyme Judgment

Read each set of words aloud. Ask the child to tell you which word rhymes with the first word.

1. third — bird — fort
2. seat — treat — breeze
3. clean — green — can
4. mix — hats — sticks
5. town — frown — sun
6. flour — dinner — hour
7. stripe — rope — pipe
8. trip — slip — pop
9. hide — road — side
10. land — band — find
11. ring — wing — song
12. more — her — roar
13. park — shark — shirt
14. tank — string — bank
15. scream — dream — seen
16. cold — bold — cone
17. Mark — dark — smoke
18. floor — scar — door
19. room — book — broom
20. letter — sweater — lemon

Odd One Out

Rhyme Judgment

Here is a list of words to refer to when completing the activities on pages 34-38.

Odd One Out 1, page 34

1. hat   deer   cat
2. boat   coat   spoon
3. three mop   top
4. rain   train   ear
5. crown shell   bell

Odd One Out 2, page 35

1. pan   bed   fan
2. sun   tail   one
3. whale sail   man
4. map   gate   skate
5. ice   dice   goat

Odd One Out 3, page 36

1. sock   bee   clock
2. car   two   shoe
3. bell   pig   wig
4. knee   bee   door
5. eye   tie   gate

Odd One Out 4, page 37

1. wing   rat   king
2. toe   hook   book
3. cake   lake   fire
4. log   leg   frog
5. lamp   stick   kick

Odd One Out 5, page 38

1. sled   duck   bread
2. jail   pool   school
3. corn   horn   sun
4. bow   shoe   snow
5. bug   rug   pig

Sounds Abound

33

Copyright © 1993 LinguiSystems, Inc.

Odd One Out 1

Name _____

Put an X on the picture in each row that doesn't rhyme with the others.

1.
2.
3.
4.
5.

Sounds Abound — 34 — Copyright © 1993 LinguiSystems, Inc.

Odd One Out 2

Name _____

Draw a line through the picture in each row that doesn't rhyme with the others.

1.
2.
3.
4.
5.

Sounds Abound

35

Copyright © 1993 LinguiSystems, Inc.

Odd One Out 3

Name _____

Draw a circle around the picture in each row that doesn't rhyme with the others.

1.	sock	fly	clock
2.	car	2	shoe/boot
3.	bell	pig	wig
4.	knee	fly	door
5.	eye	tie	gate

Sounds Abound   36   Copyright © 1993 LinguiSystems, Inc.

Odd One Out 4

Name _____

Color the picture in each row that doesn't rhyme with the others.

Sounds Abound   37   Copyright © 1993 LinguiSystems, Inc.

Odd One Out 5

Name _____

Put an X on the picture in each row that doesn't rhyme with the others.

1.
2.
3.
4.
5.

Sounds Abound

38

Copyright © 1993 LinguiSystems, Inc.

Odd One Out 6

Rhyme Judgment

Read each set of words aloud. Ask the child to tell you which word doesn't rhyme with the other two.

1. mad   go   had
2. time   dime   snow
3. eye   wall   small
4. same   came   duck
5. camp   bread   lamp
6. mop   fold   told
7. ran   two   plan
8. Jell-O   yellow   today
9. goat   ship   rip
10. band   tail   land
11. cat   plane   brain
12. real   steal   bat
13. wife   life   gate
14. bubble   funny   money
15. weed   pan   seed
16. dog   frog   tan
17. beep   sleep   rain
18. fight   cart   night
19. hop   shop   leg
20. rock   dock   brown

Sounds Abound

Odd One Out 7

Rhyme Judgment

Read each set of words aloud. Ask the child to tell you which word doesn't rhyme with the other two.

1. space   face   town
2. heat   jar   neat
3. doctor   wishing   fishing
4. sail   pat   bat
5. kittens   teacher   mittens
6. bowl   hole   rake
7. toe   dent   went
8. rob   job   lake
9. cab   pie   stab
10. rock   flag   knock
11. tractor   money   bunny
12. some   gum   frog
13. land   shape   grape
14. chop   pop   bug
15. no   heart   low
16. wall   ball   John
17. dry   spy   see
18. moon   spice   rice
19. clip   told   slip
20. mold   old   lake

Sounds Abound

Odd One Out 8

Rhyme Judgment

Read each set of words aloud. Ask the child to tell you which word doesn't rhyme with the other two.

1. mop   run   fun
2. part brick start
3. shut hut   sound
4. chain red   bed
5. cool lamp   rule
6. care share bee
7. rose cone   hose
8. work shirt dirt
9. trail mail   days
10. buy find   kind
11. hug fun   dug
12. rain cage   page
13. save brave made
14. skin wish   pin
15. tag wag   cat
16. ants pants sat
17. keep ship   sleep
18. bike like   trick
19. dress nice twice
20. match switch pitch

Odd One Out 9

Rhyme Judgment

Read each set of words aloud. Ask the child to tell you which word doesn't rhyme with the other two.

1. heart   park   dark
2. crash   snack   trash
3. draw   saw   caught
4. cone   joke   stone
5. sail   gray   way
6. sneak   heat   week
7. glue   new   pool
8. trip   sick   kick
9. tie   fly   night
10. wet   neck   check
11. tree   peel   free
12. gate   change   late
13. break   shake   jail
14. fire   tight   night
15. give   live   wife
16. hide   slide   sad
17. dig   jog   hog
18. flag   pig   drag
19. jump   stamp   dump
20. rack   dark   park

Sounds Abound   Copyright © 1993 LinguiSystems, Inc.

Fun With Rhymes

Rhyme Production

Have the child listen as you read the following rhymes aloud. Then, have him complete the rhymes with rhyming words.

1. A fish named Jim, was learning to ___.
   (swim)

2. A little girl named Mandy, got sick from eating too much ___.
   (candy)

3. The little star, way up high, was the brightest star in the ___.
   (sky)

4. Buzza, buzza went the bee, stay far away and don't sting ___.
   (me)

5. Squeak, squeak says the mouse, as he runs through the ___.
   (house)

6. When Jordan grows up, he'll be a cook. When Jose grows up, he'll write a ___.
   (book)

7. Three gray elephants went out in a boat. They were so heavy, it couldn't ___.
   (float)

8. If I were able to fly to Mars, I'd take lots of pictures of the ___.
   (stars)

9. When my friend Angela spends the night, sometimes we giggle. Sometimes we ___.
   (fight)

10. Clickety, clack, clickety, clack, the train went roaring down the ___.
    (track)

11. Moo cow, moo cow eating hay, give us lots of milk ___.
    (today)

12. There goes Mario. There goes Mike. I'm going with them to ride my ___.
    (bike)

Now, have the child say the rhymes with you.

Sounds Abound

Fun With Rhymes

Rhyme Production

Have the child listen as you read the following rhymes aloud. Then, have her complete the rhymes with rhyming words.

1. The wooly worm crawled with a wiggle. He was so cute, he made me ____.
   (giggle)

2. Skitter, skitter, skee, the squirrel ran up the ____.
   (tree)

3. I went to the garden to help Dad rake. And jumped three feet when I saw a ____.
   (snake)

4. The lady wore a dress of red. With a matching hat upon her ____.
   (head)

5. First I was seven, then I was eight. Soon I'll be nine, and I can't ____.
   (wait)

6. "Gobble," said the turkey, "fiddle-dee-dee." No one's making a dinner out of ____.
   (me)

7. Oatmeal and raisin cookies are yummy. Just what I need to fill my ____.
   (tummy)

8. The clown stepped back and threw a pie. It hit a man in the ____.
   (eye)

9. I wish that I could write a song. Not too short, and not too ____.
   (long)

10. My shoes, my shoes, they're way too tight. I need a pair that fits just ____.
    (right)

11. He dug the potatoes and filled the sack. Just lifting it would break your ____.
    (back)

12. The bear went shopping for some honey. But he forgot to take his ____.
    (money)

Now, have the child say the rhymes with you.

* The same activities can be done using rhymes from the suggested Sound Awareness Books listed on pages 9-12.

Make a Rhyme

Rhyme Production

Here is a list of words to refer to when completing the activities on pages 46-50.

Make a Rhyme 1, page 46

1. king — ring
2. bat — hat
3. jail — snail
4. deer — ear
5. tie — pie

Make a Rhyme 2, page 47

1. bee — three
2. hair — bear
3. bow — snow
4. gate — plate
5. bed — sled

Make a Rhyme 3, page 48

1. sun — one
2. book — hook
3. car — jar
4. dice — ice
5. dog — log

Make a Rhyme 4, page 49

1. goat — boat
2. box — rocks
3. hose — toes
4. rake — lake
5. can — man

Make a Rhyme 5, page 50

1. bag — flag
2. door — four
3. clock — sock
4. mop — stop
5. pig — wig

Make a Rhyme 1   Name _____

Write a word or draw a picture in the box that rhymes with the other pictures in the row.

1.		
2.		
3.		
4.		
5.		

Sounds Abound　　　　　　　46　　　　　　　Copyright © 1993 LinguiSystems, Inc.

Make a Rhyme 2

Name _____

Write a word or draw a picture in the box that rhymes with the other pictures in the row.

1.			
2.			
3.			
4.			
5.			

Sounds Abound   47   Copyright © 1993 LinguiSystems, Inc

Make a Rhyme 3

Name _____

Write a word or draw a picture in the box that rhymes with the other pictures in the row.

1.	sun	1	
2.	book	hook	
3.	car	band-aid	
4.	dice	ice	
5.	dog	log	

Sounds Abound   48   Copyright © 1993 LinguiSystems, Inc.

Make a Rhyme 4   Name _____

Write a word or draw a picture in the box that rhymes with the other pictures in the row.

1.	goat	boat	
2.	box	rocks	
3.	hose	toes	
4.	rake	lake	
5.	soup	(old man)	

Sounds Abound   49   Copyright © 1993 LinguiSystems, Inc

Make a Rhyme 5   Name _____

Write a word or draw a picture in the box that rhymes with the other pictures in the row.

1.	bag / flag	
2.	door / 4	
3.	clock / sock	
4.	mop / stop	
5.	pig / wig	

Sounds Abound   50   Copyright © 1993 LinguiSystems, Inc.

Make a Rhyme 6

Rhyme Production

Read the words in each row aloud. Ask the child to think of a word that rhymes with these words.

1.	snow	Joe	21.	lump	hump
2.	fight	white	22.	shook	hook
3.	sling	thing	23.	wish	dish
4.	three	he	24.	tune	soon
5.	rail	fail	25.	seen	screen
6.	shed	fed	26.	thin	spin
7.	shy	try	27.	got	shot
8.	done	none	28.	suit	fruit
9.	clay	way	29.	blade	grade
10.	pair	wear	30.	fall	hall
11.	break	wake	31.	crown	gown
12.	crop	flop	32.	same	tame
13.	knock	flock	33.	jog	fog
14.	true	new	34.	sang	rang
15.	thumb	hum	35.	date	late
16.	cub	tub	36.	wag	brag
17.	leap	sweep	37.	mound	found
18.	bear	tear	38.	shirt	Burt
19.	meat	feet	39.	not	dot
20.	tar	bar	40.	shock	dock

Sounds Abound

Make a Rhyme 7

Rhyme Production

Read the words in each row aloud. Ask the child to think of a word that rhymes with the two words given.

1. blink — stink
2. seem — steam
3. mole — scroll
4. beak — leak
5. feed — speed
6. lace — space
7. wag — rag
8. damp — stamp
9. jug — mug
10. hire — dryer
11. job — knob
12. sold — mold
13. poke — broke
14. but — hut
15. torn — worn
16. book — look
17. skin — pin
18. top — mop
19. shoe — flew
20. Jan — tan
21. Mike — strike
22. close — toes
23. joy — Roy
24. float — wrote
25. stool — fool
26. bad — had
27. tone — stone
28. chalk — walk
29. trees — please
30. crime — dime
31. when — hen
32. bricks — tricks
33. mouse — house
34. peg — beg
35. lean — keen
36. Mark — spark
37. jar — car
38. bread — Ted
39. note — tote
40. one — bun

Sounds Abound

Copyright © 1993 LinguiSystems, Inc.

Make More Rhymes

Rhyme Production

Here is a list of words to refer to when completing the activities on pages 54-58.

Make More Rhymes 1, page 54

1. cat
2. cake
3. ear
4. feet
5. fan

Make More Rhymes 2, page 55

1. rug
2. eye
3. log
4. knee
5. toe

Make More Rhymes 3, page 56

1. sock
2. ball
3. sun
4. sheep
5. nose

Make More Rhymes 4, page 57

1. wheel
2. boy
3. nail
4. bear
5. kite

Make More Rhymes 5, page 58

1. book
2. hand
3. net
4. nest
5. ring

Make More Rhymes 1   Name _____

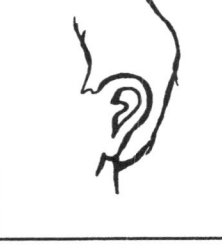

Think of as many words as you can that rhyme with the pictures in the boxes.
Write the words or draw pictures of them on the lines.

1.

2.

3.

4.

5.

Sounds Abound   54   Copyright © 1993 LinguiSystems, Inc.

Make More Rhymes 2   Name _____

Think of as many words as you can that rhyme with the pictures in the boxes.
Write the words or draw pictures of them on the lines.

1.

2.

3.

4.

5.

Sounds Abound   55   Copyright © 1993 LinguiSystems, Inc

Make More Rhymes 3   Name _____

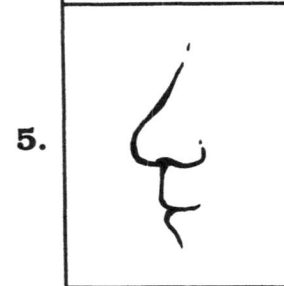

Think of as many words as you can that rhyme with the pictures in the boxes.
Write the words or draw pictures of them on the lines.

1. 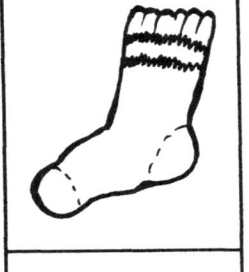 [sock] _____ _____ _____ _____ _____

2.  [ball] _____ _____ _____ _____ _____

3. 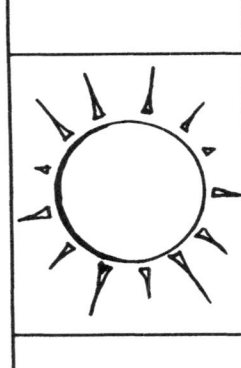 [sun] _____ _____ _____ _____ _____

4.  [sheep] _____ _____ _____ _____ _____

5. [nose] _____ _____ _____ _____ _____

Sounds Abound   56   Copyright © 1993 LinguiSystems, Inc.

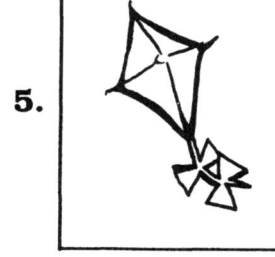

Make More Rhymes 4   Name _____

Think of as many words as you can that rhyme with the pictures in the boxes.
Write the words or draw pictures of them on the lines.

1. 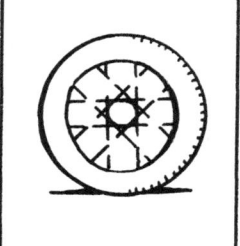 [tire]

2. [boy]

3.  [nail]

4.  [bear]

5. [kite]

Sounds Abound   57   Copyright © 1993 LinguiSystems, Inc

Make More Rhymes 5   Name _____

Think of as many words as you can that rhyme with the pictures in the boxes.
Write the words or draw pictures of them on the lines.

1.	book
2.	hand
3.	net
4.	nest
5.	ring

Sounds Abound   58   Copyright © 1993 LinguiSystems, Inc.

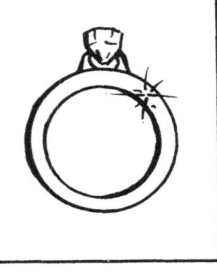

Make More Rhymes 6

Rhyme Production

Read the words aloud. Then, ask the child to tell you as many words as he can that rhyme with the word you say.

1. make
2. by
3. so
4. hear
5. do
6. cave
7. hop
8. bring
9. day
10. pack
11. tan
12. rail
13. sat
14. tall
15. stand
16. bear
17. fit
18. mat
19. race
20. pick

21. might
22. bar
23. hate
24. peel
25. glad
26. keep
27. smell
28. let
29. cent
30. hip
31. rest
32. price
33. seat
34. wide
35. wig
36. lunch
37. clip
38. sew
39. sack
40. more

Sounds Abound   59   Copyright © 1993 LinguiSystems, Inc.

Make More Rhymes 7

Rhyme Production

Read the words aloud. Then, ask the child to tell you as many words as she can that rhyme with the word you say.

1. lap
2. fill
3. tool
4. wheel
5. bit
6. shock
7. hog
8. pick
9. not
10. wink
11. tug
12. bun
13. bark
14. shape
15. said
16. Meg
17. bag
18. rice
19. lake
20. dry

21. bean
22. stand
23. bite
24. took
25. fair
26. blocks
27. note
28. cash
29. tore
30. frown
31. bricks
32. grown
33. coal
34. seem
35. drain
36. bend
37. cool
38. hose
39. joke
40. four

Sounds Abound

Copyright © 1993 LinguiSystems, Inc.

Going on a Trip

Rhyme Play

On the next page, you'll find pictures that rhyme. Cut out the pictures and mix them up. Place the pictures in front of the child right side up.

Tell the child to pick up a picture and find its rhyming mate. Next, have the child decide which one he would take on a trip. Then, have him glue this picture onto the suitcase.

Going on a Trip

Rhyme Play

A Rhyming Song

Rhyme Play

Yopp (1990) has adapted the following rhyming song which is sung to the tune of "Jimmy Cracked Corn." Sing the song together. Next, ask a child to give rhyming words for the target word heard in the song. Then, incorporate the rhyming words into the song:

Who has a word that rhymes with *hat*?
Who has a word that rhymes with *hat*?
Who has a word that rhymes with *hat*?
It must rhyme with *hat!*

If a child responded with *cat*, the following could be sung:

Cat is a word that rhymes with *hat*.
Cat is a word that rhymes with *hat*.
Cat is a word that rhymes with *hat*.
Cat rhymes with *hat!*

Other possible responses might include:

at	bat
fat	gnat
mat	pat
sat	rat

Listed below are other possible target and rhyming words:

shell: sell, tell, bell, smell, spell, fell, well, yell
hide: ride, slide, tide, wide, bride, pride, side
kite: white, might, night, sight, light, fight, bright, bite, tight
row: bow, no, snow, sew, low, toe, blow, foe, go, hoe, mow
fun: one, sun, done, bun, run, pun, ton

For more fun, have the children generate some of their own words.

Sounds Abound

I Spy

Rhyme Play

Use the words in the boxes below with the scenes on pages 65-67. Say to the child, "I spy with my little eye, a word that rhymes with . . . ." Complete the sentence using a word from the box. Next, have the child find the picture of the rhyming word in the scene and circle it. Then, ask the child to think of another word that rhymes with the word you said. Do this with each word in the box.

At a Parade, *page 65*

down	bat
sand	log
dragon	dandy
luck	gum
jar	force

In Your Room, *page 66*

look	sock
red	two
tall	bear
ramp	four
coat	willow

At the Farm, *page 67*

big	leg
now	fog
yarn	hat
keep	cake
sense	day

At a Parade

Name _____

Sounds Abound

In Your Room

Name _____

Name _____

At the Farm

Play Ball

Rhyme Play

Have the children sit in a circle. Next, say a word that has several words that can rhyme with it. Then, toss a ball to one of the children. Have that child say a word that rhymes with the word you said. Then, have her toss the ball to someone else. Start with a new word each time the children run out of rhyming words. Below are examples of words that work well with this activity.

pie	bye	eye	sigh
	cry	high	tie
	die	my	why
go	bow	hoe	row
	blow	Joe	snow
	crow	low	so
	dough	mow	tow
	foe	no	whoa
cake	ache	Jake	sake
	bake	lake	snake
	fake	make	take
	flake	rake	wake
bear	air	fair	rare
	chair	mare	wear
	dare	pair	tear
feet	beat	heat	seat
	eat	meat	sleet
	fleet	neat	sweet
	greet	wheat	treat
tea	bee	flea	key
	see	free	knee
	gee	Lee	fee
	me	we	he

Variation: Have partners toss a ball back and forth while naming word pairs.

Sounds Abound

Rhyming Charades

Rhyme Play

Copy pictures from the previous rhyming sections. Glue these pictures on index cards. Then, take turns with the child choosing a card and acting out a word that rhymes with the picture on the card. For example, if the card has a picture of a stick, the child could act out the word *kick*.

Rhyme Pretest

Evaluation

This pretest uses the Odd One Out format. There are three training items. Use the pictures from pages 34-38 as training items for the child who can't perform correctly on any of the training items provided. Correct answers should only be given on the training items.

Read each set of words aloud. Then, ask the child to choose the word that doesn't rhyme with the other two words.

Training Items

1. bad   wash   sad
2. game   name   house
3. hand   day   say

Test Items

1. year   doll   near
2. feed   weed   spoon
3. pie   tell   fell
4. jet   pet   ball
5. mice   snake   rice
6. tree   ride   side
7. bean   sun   clean
8. gold   sold   bed
9. gum   time   dime
10. light   hat   right

Rhyme Posttest *Evaluation*

This posttest uses the Odd One Out format. There are three training items. Correct answers should only be given on the training items.

Read each set of words aloud. Then, ask the child to choose the word that doesn't rhyme with the other two words.

Training Items

1. fan   hill   pill
2. chip   nail   lip
3. cut   nut   bird

Test Items

1. nose   pot   dot
2. net   chair   bet
3. back   day   sack
4. jeep   sheep   rain
5. bowl   face   race
6. Coke   joke   girl
7. bone   can   phone
8. whale   fall   mall
9. dish   fish   bush
10. toad   food   road

Beginnings and Endings

One of the earliest signs of children's awareness of phonemes or individual speech sounds is their understanding that words begin or end with the same sound. This awareness plays an important part in children learning the association between sounds and letters.

This section on beginnings and endings has activities to help children become aware of the phonemes in speech. It's divided into the following three parts: sound judgment, sound production, and sound play.

- In the sound judgment activities, children are asked to make judgments about whether or not words begin or end with the same sound.

- In the sound production activities, children are asked to say words with the same beginning sounds as the target words.

- In the sound play activities, children play games and sing songs to practice saying words with the same sounds.

Activities with pictures are used initially in both the sound judgment and sound production activities. These activities are followed by word lists to be read aloud to children.

Sound Pairs?

Sound Judgment

Here is a list of words to refer to when completing the activities on pages 74-79.

Sound Pairs? 1, page 74

1. bell — bow
2. sun — sock
3. king — pig
4. dog — deer
5. lake — girl

Sound Pairs? 2, page 75

1. fin — feet
2. jail — hat
3. rug — rake
4. pan — pig
5. boat — pie

Sound Pairs? 3, page 76

1. shoe — shell
2. toes — door
3. log — light
4. chair — cheese
5. goat — can

Sound Pairs? 4, page 77

1. cat — nut
2. dice — house
3. bear — light
4. dog — pig
5. mop — sheep

Sound Pairs? 5, page 78

1. pool — knee
2. jail — wheel
3. jar — rock
4. sun — horn
5. sink — truck

Sound Pairs? 6, page 79

1. leg — stick
2. gate — boat
3. sun — can
4. hat — light
5. coat — corn

Sounds Abound

Sound Pairs? 1

Name _____

Name the pictures in each row. If the words begin with the same sound, draw circles around each picture.

1.
2.
3.
4.
5.

Sounds Abound   74   Copyright © 1993 LinguiSystems, Inc.

Sound Pairs? 2

Name _____

Name the pictures in each row. If the words begin with the same sound, draw an X on each picture.

1.
2.
3.
4.
5.

Sounds Abound   75   Copyright © 1993 LinguiSystems, Inc.

Sound Pairs? 3

Name _____

Name the pictures in each row. If the words begin with the same sound, draw a line through each picture.

1.	boot	shell
2.	foot	door
3.	log	light
4.	chair	cheese
5.	goat	soup

Sounds Abound 76 Copyright © 1993 LinguiSystems, Inc.

Sound Pairs? 4   Name _____

Name the pictures in each row. If the words end with the same sound, clap your hands.

1.	cat	peanut
2.	dice	house
3.	bear	lightbulb
4.	dog	pig
5.	mop	sheep

Sounds Abound   77   Copyright © 1993 LinguiSystems, Inc.

Sound Pairs? 5

Name _____

Name the pictures in each row. If the words end with the same sound, draw a circle around each picture.

1.
2.
3.
4.
5.

Sounds Abound   78   Copyright © 1993 LinguiSystems, Inc.

Sound Pairs? 6

Name _____

Name the pictures in each row. If the words end with the same sound, draw a line through each picture.

1.	leg	stick
2.	gate	boat
3.	sun	can
4.	hat	light
5.	coat	corn

Sounds Abound   79   Copyright © 1993 LinguiSystems, Inc.

Sound Pairs? 7

Sound Judgment

Read each word pair aloud. Ask the child to tell you if the two words begin with the same sound.

1.	bake	bone	21.	choose	chop
2.	dot	deer	22.	van	vest
3.	weed	gift	23.	sit	zoo
4.	fun	fur	24.	gate	gold
5.	hold	card	25.	Coke	gift
6.	lip	lost	26.	bake	bear
7.	men	mouse	27.	raft	road
8.	shake	tie	28.	nose	mask
9.	now	nurse	29.	toast	ten
10.	post	point	30.	time	down
11.	loud	sew	31.	blood	please
12.	sick	see	32.	catch	car
13.	tub	tongue	33.	right	ring
14.	ship	shake	34.	ghost	give
15.	use	tail	35.	vase	fire
16.	wash	wood	36.	head	hole
17.	chair	choke	37.	jump	jug
18.	cheese	bow	38.	dip	talk
19.	thick	thank	39.	hurt	high
20.	joke	jar	40.	you	yawn

Sounds Abound

Copyright © 1993 LinguiSystems, Inc.

Sound Pairs? 8

Sound Judgment

Read each word pair aloud. Ask the child to tell you if the two words end with the same sound.

1.	shop	soap		21.	beach	itch
2.	hat	pin		22.	dance	piece
3.	web	bib		23.	wash	reach
4.	move	love		24.	bridge	age
5.	lip	mess		25.	tough	face
6.	fall	hill		26.	fuzz	peas
7.	lake	snow		27.	mud	red
8.	swim	lamb		28.	road	wait
9.	off	leaf		29.	fish	leash
10.	mouth	bath		30.	fun	name
11.	fast	well		31.	tub	pipe
12.	pan	win		32.	sit	hat
13.	smooth	breathe		33.	bike	pink
14.	shell	small		34.	witch	catch
15.	work	song		35.	mouse	rose
16.	live	boat		36.	duck	shake
17.	game	farm		37.	race	pass
18.	long	sad		38.	bug	lake
19.	build	paid		39.	ring	strong
20.	kite	paint		40.	bag	rug

Sounds Abound

Copyright © 1993 LinguiSystems, Inc.

Match 'Em Up

Sound Judgment

Here is a list of words to refer to when completing the activities on pages 84-89.

Match 'Em Up 1, page 84

1.	bug	ring	bed
2.	tent	tack	bear
3.	door	dog	hook
4.	fan	wig	feet
5.	sail	sink	four

Match 'Em Up 2, page 85

1.	log	cat	lake
2.	snail	three	snow
3.	mop	map	wheel
4.	pie	kite	pin
5.	rock	rug	boy

Match 'Em Up 3, page 86

1.	seal	net	sand
2.	bee	man	book
3.	pan	pool	bed
4.	king	sun	corn
5.	nose	dice	nest

Sounds Abound

Match 'Em Up

Sound Judgment

Match 'Em Up 4, page 87

1. top   map   boy
2. shave   hand   glove
3. moon   log   pan
4. school   nail   shoe
5. boat   jar   kite

Match 'Em Up 5, page 88

1. mouse   bus   ball
2. bed   slide   dice
3. cheese   sink   hose
4. tail   shell   hat
5. fish   cat   brush

Match 'Em Up 6, page 89

1. rake   brick   hose
2. dog   bed   leg
3. skate   sled   coat
4. duck   sock   pig
5. sun   drum   fan

Match 'Em Up 1   Name _____

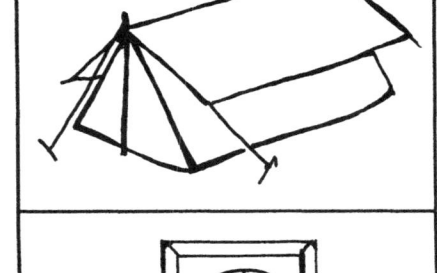

Listen as your teacher names the pictures in each row. Then, put an X on the picture that begins with the same sound as the first word.

1.
2.
3.
4.
5.

Sounds Abound   84   Copyright © 1993 LinguiSystems, Inc.

Match 'Em Up 2   Name _____

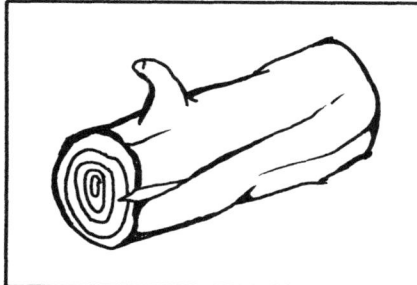

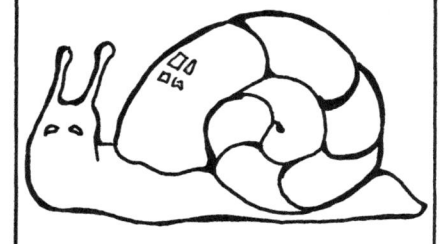

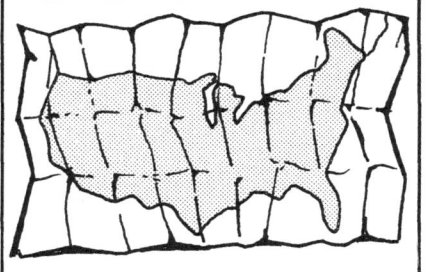

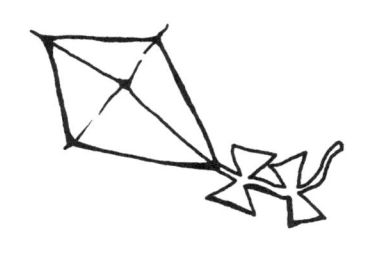

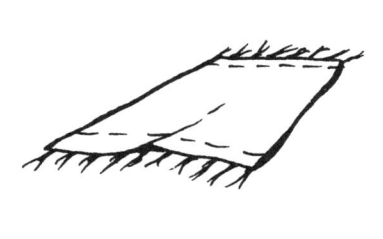

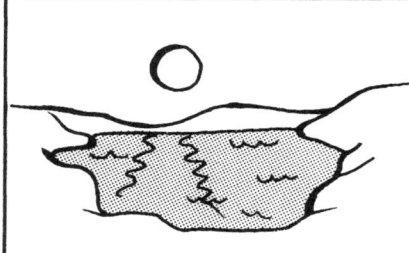

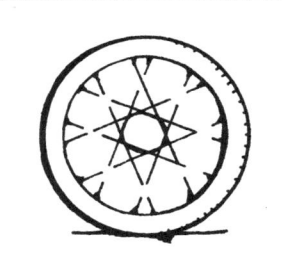

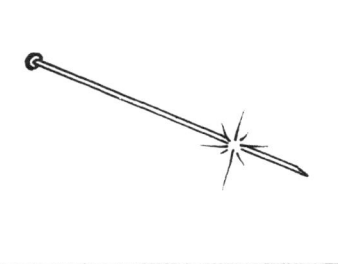

Listen as your teacher names the pictures in each row. Then, circle the picture that begins with the same sound as the first word.

1.
2.
3.
4.
5.

Sounds Abound   85   Copyright © 1993 LinguiSystems, Inc.

Match 'Em Up 3   Name _____

Listen as your teacher names the pictures in each row. Then, draw a line through the picture that begins with the same sound as the first word.

1.
2.
3.
4.
5.

Sounds Abound   86   Copyright © 1993 LinguiSystems, Inc.

Match 'Em Up 4   Name _____

Listen as your teacher names the pictures in each row. Then, color the picture that ends with the same sound as the first word.

1.
2.
3.
4.
5.

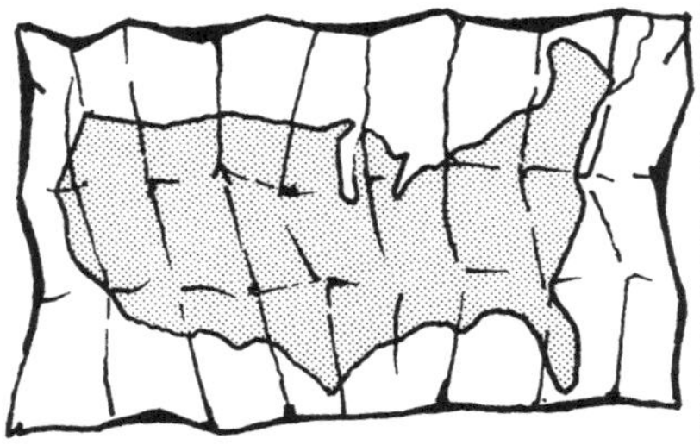

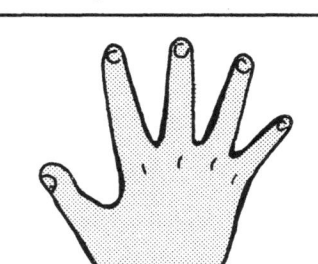

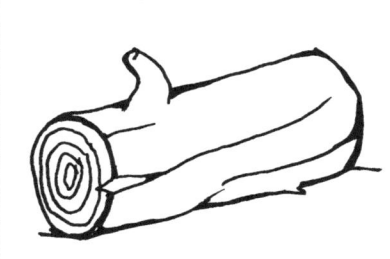

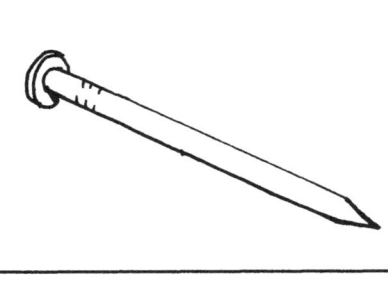

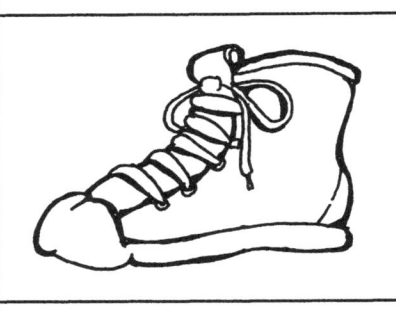

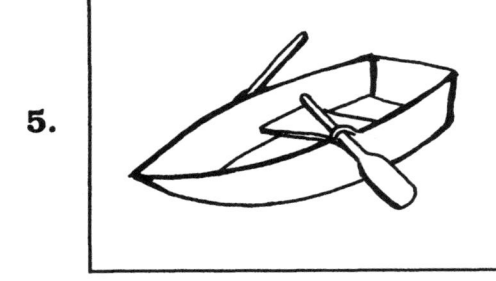

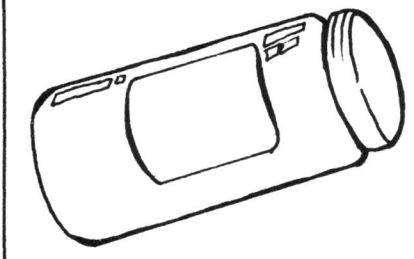

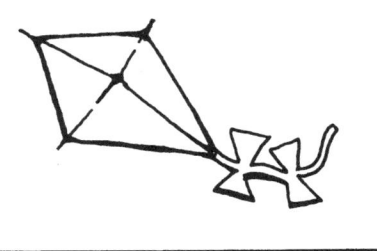

Sounds Abound   87   Copyright © 1993 LinguiSystems, Inc.

Match 'Em Up 5   Name _____

Listen as your teacher names the pictures in each row.   Then, put an X on the picture that ends with the same sound as the first word.

Sounds Abound   88   Copyright © 1993 LinguiSystems, Inc.

Match 'Em Up 6   Name _____

Listen as your teacher names the pictures in each row. Then, circle the picture that ends with the same sound as the first word.

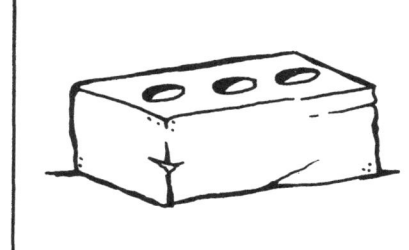

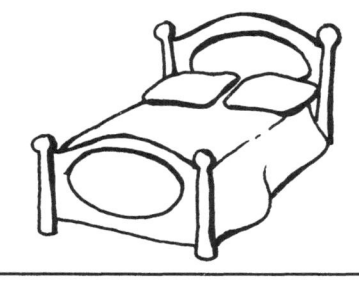

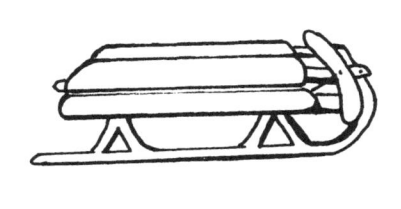

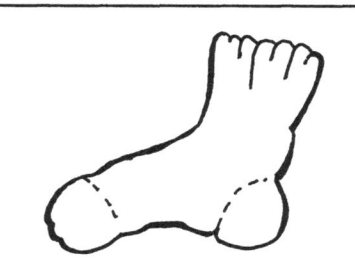

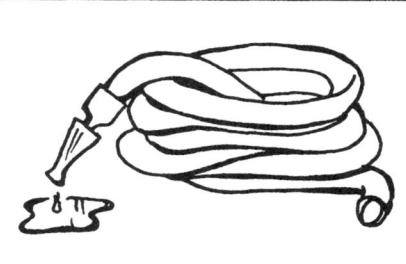

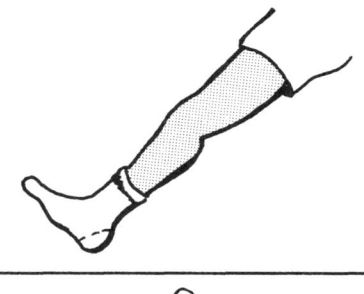

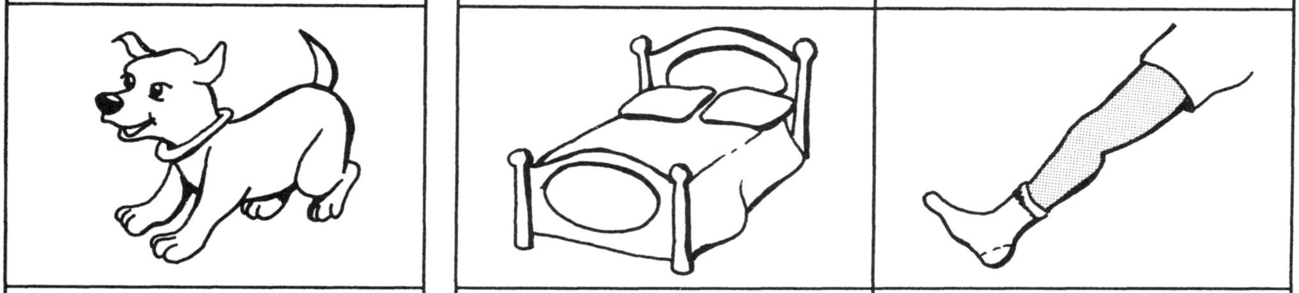

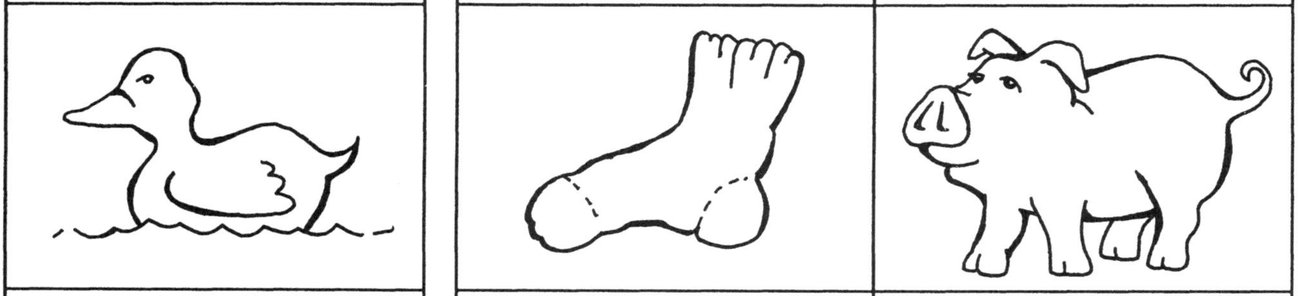

Sounds Abound   89   Copyright © 1993 LinguiSystems, Inc.

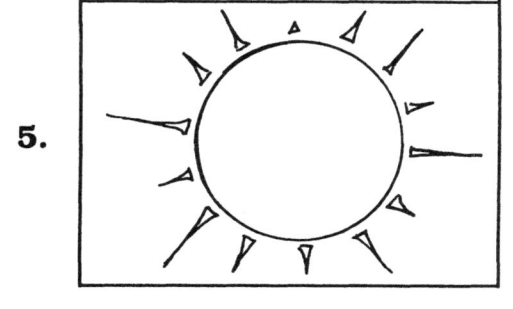

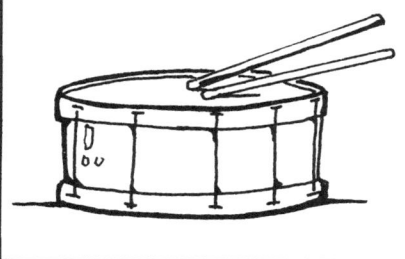

Match 'Em Up 7

Sound Judgment

Read each set of words aloud. Ask the child to tell you which word begins with the same sound as the first word.

1. did   dirt   peel
2. first   year   fine
3. last   like   pear
4. more   coat   mud
5. next   hide   nap
6. bill   band   send
7. team   toad   four
8. dish   fear   dive
9. feel   food   wear
10. worm   light   wind
11. pot   pink   cars
12. real   ride   find
13. seat   wall   sound
14. fat   field   cash
15. went   hear   well
16. should   shop   fist
17. yawn   dad   your
18. they   cup   that
19. head   hill   six
20. sew   cone   side

Sounds Abound — 90 — Copyright © 1993 LinguiSystems, Inc.

Match 'Em Up 8

Sound Judgment

Read each set of words aloud. Ask the child to tell you which word begins with the same sound as the first word.

1.	price	block	print
2.	kiss	kind	done
3.	good	goose	new
4.	ten	nut	tub
5.	bank	belt	make
6.	sad	zip	sign
7.	shape	chips	short
8.	teach	turn	dark
9.	want	rug	wood
10.	bite	board	pay
11.	chin	jog	chief
12.	milk	meet	pipe
13.	not	name	tall
14.	pain	bar	patch
15.	neat	milk	neck
16.	glass	clap	glue
17.	green	grill	cry
18.	frown	vase	fry
19.	climb	clean	glow
20.	star	step	school

Sounds Abound   91   Copyright © 1993 LinguiSystems, Inc.

Match 'Em Up 9

Sound Judgment

Read each set of words aloud. Ask the child to tell you which word ends with the same sound as the first word.

1.	chop	town	map
2.	grab	robe	hall
3.	time	worm	ride
4.	knife	team	roof
5.	give	dive	car
6.	hole	fight	smile
7.	teeth	rake	both
8.	rain	ship	brown
9.	dip	jump	small
10.	tub	door	cab
11.	name	drum	lake
12.	bean	step	down
13.	wife	laugh	kite
14.	shave	sand	five
15.	school	hook	dial
16.	house	face	rub
17.	gate	push	foot
18.	noise	prize	spoon
19.	child	cold	race
20.	call	fill	gum

Sounds Abound   Copyright © 1993 LinguiSystems, Inc.

Match 'Em Up 10

Sound Judgment

Read each set of words aloud. Ask the child to tell you which word ends with the same sound as the first word.

1.	bank	run	cork
2.	night	push	cat
3.	string	long	cough
4.	bake	face	clock
5.	jog	close	leg
6.	lunch	itch	fruit
7.	lock	pack	wave
8.	clean	men	dime
9.	log	trash	pig
10.	bush	splash	ice
11.	lose	crash	nose
12.	climb	learn	dream
13.	bus	kiss	leaf
14.	jet	kick	right
15.	duck	shake	wing
16.	feed	card	pet
17.	bug	head	egg
18.	grape	soap	light
19.	lick	sit	desk
20.	safe	leaf	house

Sounds Abound

Odd One Out

Sound Judgment

Here is a list of words to refer to when completing the activities on pages 96-101.

Odd One Out 1, page 96

1. bear   hose   ball
2. sink   door   dart
3. four   fire   pool
4. corn   lamp   leg
5. sink   bell   socks

Odd One Out 2, page 97

1. one   shoe   wing
2. fox   fan   wig
3. pan   leg   lake
4. chain   chair   rock
5. rain   heart   rake

Odd One Out 3, page 98

1. bed   pie   pin
2. duck   dice   toe
3. jar   cheese jail
4. gate   girl   cow
5. nail   mop   nest

Odd One Out

Sound Judgment

Odd One Out 4, page 99

1. stop   cow   lamp
2. hat   boat   door
3. snow   hand   bed
4. stamp   sheep   leg
5. rain   bell   girl

Odd One Out 5, page 100

1. fan   tack   clown
2. goat   four   kite
3. house   ice   pie
4. jail   tire   pool
5. clock   hook   bone

Odd One Out 6, page 101

1. nail   foot   wheel
2. owl   flag   egg
3. drum   moon   fan
4. nose   bees   fish
5. cake   truck   dog

Odd One Out 1   Name _____

Name the pictures in each row. Then, put an X on the picture that doesn't begin with the same sound as the others.

1. bear | hose | ball
2. sink | door | dart
3. 4 | fire | pool
4. corn | lamp | leg
5. sink | bell | sock

Sounds Abound   96   Copyright © 1993 LinguiSystems, Inc.

Odd One Out 2

Name _____

Name the pictures in each row. Then, put a line through the picture that doesn't begin with the same sound as the others.

1.
2.
3.
4.
5.

Sounds Abound   97   Copyright © 1993 LinguiSystems, Inc.

Odd One Out 3   Name _____

Name the pictures in each row. Then, circle the picture that doesn't begin with the same sound as the others.

1. bed | pie | wand
2. duck | dice | thumb
3. jar | cheese | jail
4. gate | girl | cow
5. nail | mop | nest

Odd One Out 4

Name _____

Name the pictures in each row. Then, color the picture that doesn't end with the same sound as the others.

1.
2.
3.
4.
5.

Sounds Abound · 99 · Copyright © 1993 LinguiSystems, Inc.

Odd One Out 5

Name _____

Name the pictures in each row. Then, put an X on the picture that doesn't end with the same sound as the others.

1.
2.
3.
4.
5.

Sounds Abound

100

Copyright © 1993 LinguiSystems, Inc.

Odd One Out 6

Name _____

Name the pictures in each row. Then, draw a line through the picture that doesn't end with the same sound as the others.

1.
2.
3.
4.
5.

Sounds Abound 101 Copyright © 1993 LinguiSystems, Inc.

Odd One Out 7

Sound Judgment

Read each set of words aloud. Ask the child to tell you which word doesn't begin with the same sound as the others.

1. boy   bear   can
2. drink   fall   farm
3. door   desk   run
4. fox   toy   food
5. leg   boy   leaf
6. ring   mask   mop
7. nail   knee   slow
8. door   park   pail
9. rain   rat   fork
10. sack   move   sink
11. green   tail   tooth
12. shark   pop   sheep
13. chips   chain   ant
14. mail   van   vest
15. web   comb   wall
16. three   throw   lip
17. wheel   hand   where
18. read   dark   date
19. zoo   zip   boot
20. lake   you   yes

Sounds Abound   Copyright © 1993 LinguiSystems, Inc.

Odd One Out 8

Sound Judgment

Read each set of words aloud. Ask the child to tell you which word doesn't begin with the same sound as the others.

1. ham turn hang
2. go rack rip
3. stop steal cow
4. break play brown
5. flip flow ghost
6. sun cry crawl
7. no most knock
8. jay germ change
9. cow good coin
10. bell page part
11. check joke cheer
12. sad safe sheep
13. vase fair face
14. march mad neck
15. blue play please
16. bread pray bring
17. small snail smart
18. bark beach pants
19. drink try true
20. blue blast play

Odd One Out 9

Sound Judgment

Read each set of words aloud. Ask the child to tell you which word doesn't end with the same sound as the others.

1. shop — pear — soap
2. web — seat — bib
3. move — love — horn
4. red — fall — hill
5. swim — lamb — dish
6. off — girl — leaf
7. coat — bath — mouth
8. pan — nap — win
9. smooth — breathe — light
10. road — shell — small
11. live — car — wave
12. dad — game — farm
13. beach — itch — fat
14. build — paid — ring
15. game — kite — paint
16. face — hide — dance
17. fuzz — peas — hot
18. mud — win — red
19. pink — fish — wash
20. bone — fight — eat

Odd One Out 10

Sound Judgment

Read each set of words aloud. Ask the child to tell you which word doesn't end with the same sound as the others.

1. block — cook — juice
2. wish — dog — rag
3. pan — bone — hide
4. couch — boat — rich
5. brush — house — crash
6. leaf — dress — mouse
7. street — net — fun
8. cat — break — hook
9. frog — hug — road
10. time — nap — swim
11. fat — bed — cloud
12. top — tub — ship
13. moon — run — gum
14. tape — mail — bowl
15. sheet — kid — spot
16. kiss — grass — fish
17. book — coat — duck
18. shark — long — king
19. brick — knock — hot
20. red — bag — dig

Sounds Abound

Same Sounds 1

Sound Production

Have the child listen as you read a sentence containing words that begin with the same sound. Then, have the child complete the sentence with a word that begins with the same sound as the other words.

1. Silly snakes sing ____. *(songs)*

2. Luiz bounces ____. *(balls)*

3. Renee likes French ____. *(fries)*

4. Gilberto hiked up the ____. *(hill)*

5. Kim cooks in the ____. *(kitchen)*

6. He honked his ____. *(horn)*

7. The chewy cookies were chocolate ____. *(chip)*

8. Nam likes to eat lima beans for ____. *(lunch)*

9. Zack saw zebras at the ____. *(zoo)*

10. Randy runs in a ____. *(race)*

11. Dora has a jar of ____. *(jelly, jelly beans, jam)*

12. Rebecca wears a ruby red ____. *(ring, rose)*

13. Lucy licks lemon ____. *(lollipops)*

14. Sean pet the ____. *(puppy, poodle, pig)*

15. Mike mopped up the mess he ____. *(made)*

Sounds Abound

Same Sounds 2

Sound Production

Have the child listen as you read a sentence containing words that begin with the same sound. Then, have the child complete the sentence with a word that begins with the same sound as the other words.

1. Wednesday, the weather was ____. *(warm, windy)*

2. She uses shampoo in the ____. *(shower)*

3. Yolanda knitted with yellow ____. *(yarn)*

4. Tim talked on the ____. *(telephone)*

5. Keesha put a penny in her ____. *(pocket)*

6. Vicki put violets in a ____. *(vase)*

7. I bought a big bunch of ____. *(bananas)*

8. Dogs dig up ____. *(dirt, dandelions)*

9. Nikki ran in the ____. *(race, road)*

10. At school, Pedro gets good ____. *(grades)*

11. Sandy sipped some hot ____. *(soup, cider)*

12. Thelma thought today was ____. *(Thursday)*

13. He helped Hanna with her ____. *(homework)*

14. Tracy tripped on the ____. *(truck)*

15. Seven ships sailed the ____. *(sea)*

Sounds Abound

Beginning Sounds

Sound Production

Here is a list of words to refer to when completing the activities on pages 109-113.

Beginning Sounds 1, page 109

1. boy   bear
2. pig   pie
3. dog   duck
4. fox   fin
5. lamp   lake

Beginning Sounds 2, page 110

1. mouse   mop
2. nut   nail
3. rain   rat
4. sock   sail
5. toes   tie

Beginning Sounds 3, page 111

1. boat   box
2. dart   deer
3. fire   four
4. log   light
5. cut   king

Beginning Sounds 4, page 112

1. man   map
2. pool   pan
3. rake   rock
4. sink   seal
5. tire   top

Beginning Sounds 5, page 113

1. knee   nest
2. can   coat
3. goat   girl
4. house   hand
5. jail   jar

Beginning Sounds 1

Name _____

Write a word or draw a picture in the box that begins with the same sound as the other words in the row.

1.	 (boy)	 (bear)	
2.	 (pig)	 (pan)	
3.	 (dog)	 (duck)	
4.	 (fox)	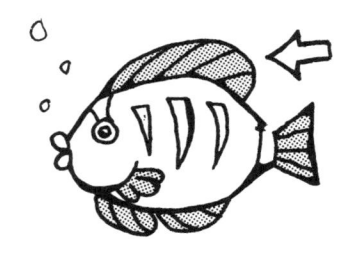 (fish)	
5.	 (lamp)	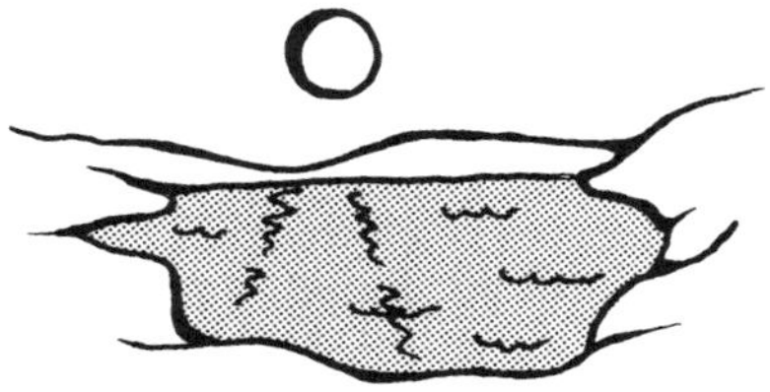 (lake)	

Sounds Abound   109   Copyright © 1993 LinguiSystems, Inc.

Beginning Sounds 2

Name _____

Write a word or draw a picture in the box that begins with the same sound as the other words in the row.

1.	mouse	mop	
2.	peanut	nail	
3.	rain	rat	
4.	sock	sail	
5.	foot	tie	

Sounds Abound   110   Copyright © 1993 LinguiSystems, Inc.

Beginning Sounds 3

Name _____

Write a word or draw a picture in the box that begins with the same sound as the other words in the row.

1.	boat	box
2.	dart	deer
3.	fire	4
4.	log	light
5.	key	king

Sounds Abound   111   Copyright © 1993 LinguiSystems, Inc.

Beginning Sounds 4   Name _____

Write a word or draw a picture in the box that begins with the same sound as the other words in the row.

1.			
2.			
3.			
4.			
5.			

Sounds Abound   112   Copyright © 1993 LinguiSystems, Inc.

Beginning Sounds 5

Name _____

Write a word or draw a picture in the box that begins with the same sound as the other words in the row.

1.	knee	nest	
2.	soup	coat	
3.	goat	girl	
4.	house	hand	
5.	jail	jar	

Sounds Abound   113   Copyright © 1993 LinguiSystems, Inc.

Beginning Sounds 6

Sound Production

Read the words in each row to the child. Ask her to tell you a word that begins with the same sound or sound blend as the two words you say.

1.	board	bank	21.	bake	beach
2.	doll	done	22.	cast	care
3.	film	fork	23.	dump	dark
4.	lid	low	24.	first	field
5.	mind	map	25.	blow	block
6.	net	night	26.	brown	breathe
7.	pie	pill	27.	flip	flake
8.	rest	rinse	28.	friend	free
9.	send	soft	29.	try	trip
10.	tease	tie	30.	stand	stir
11.	win	watch	31.	scare	skip
12.	shy	sure	32.	slip	slow
13.	chase	chair	33.	snow	sneak
14.	yes	yo-yo	34.	plane	plow
15.	cone	case	35.	cream	crown
16.	guest	gave	36.	clap	cliff
17.	here	hill	37.	green	grow
18.	job	jar	38.	glow	glad
19.	goose	gone	39.	spend	speak
20.	hop	hit	40.	drop	drip

Sounds Abound

Lots of Words

Sound Production

Here is a list of words to refer to when completing the activities on pages 116-120.

Lots of Words 1, page 116

1. ball
2. door
3. feet
4. leg
5. moon

Lots of Words 2, page 117

1. nose
2. pin
3. ring
4. sun
5. two

Lots of Words 3, page 118

1. shell
2. wheel
3. dice
4. bees
5. fan

Lots of Words 4, page 119

1. socks
2. toe
3. rug
4. nail
5. pool

Lots of Words 5, page 120

1. star
2. lake
3. car
4. gate
5. horn

Lots of Words 1   Name _____

Think of as many words as you can that begin with the same sound as the pictures in the boxes. Write the words or draw pictures of the words in the blanks next to the boxes. Then, say the words.

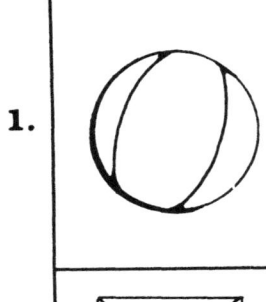

1. [ball]   _____ _____ _____ _____

2. 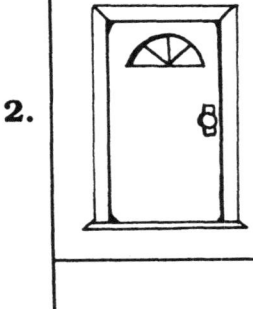 [door]   _____ _____ _____ _____

3. 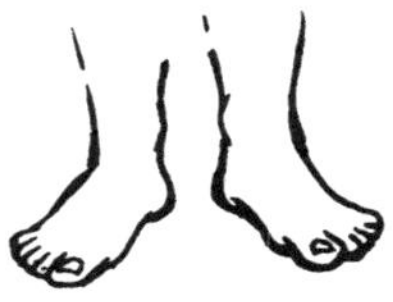 [feet]   _____ _____ _____ _____

4. 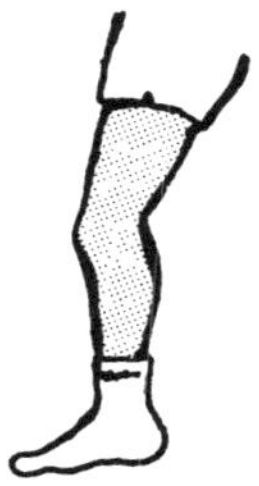 [leg]   _____ _____ _____ _____

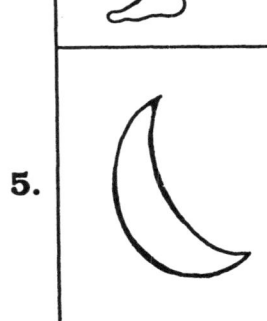

5. [moon]   _____ _____ _____ _____

Sounds Abound   116   Copyright © 1993 LinguiSystems, Inc.

Lots of Words 2   Name _____

Think of as many words as you can that begin with the same sound as the pictures in the boxes. Write the words or draw pictures of the words in the blanks next to the boxes. Then, say the words.

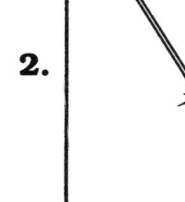

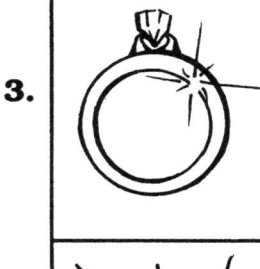

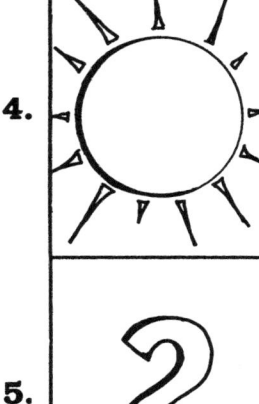

1. [nose]
_____ _____ _____ _____

2. [needle]
_____ _____ _____ _____

3. [ring]
_____ _____ _____ _____

4. [sun]
_____ _____ _____ _____

5. [2]
_____ _____ _____ _____

Sounds Abound   117   Copyright © 1993 LinguiSystems, Inc.

Lots of Words 3

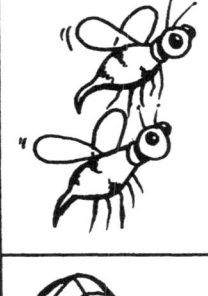

Name _____

Think of as many words as you can that begin with the same sound as the pictures in the boxes. Write the words or draw pictures of the words in the blanks next to the boxes. Then, say the words.

1. [shell]

_____ _____ _____ _____

2. [wheel]

_____ _____ _____ _____

3. [dice]

_____ _____ _____ _____

4. [mosquitoes]

_____ _____ _____ _____

5. [fan]

_____ _____ _____ _____

Sounds Abound 118 Copyright © 1993 LinguiSystems, Inc.

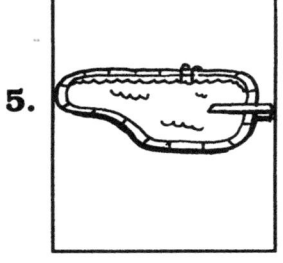

Lots of Words 4   Name_____

Think of as many words as you can that begin with the same sound as the pictures in the boxes. Write the words or draw pictures of the words in the blanks next to the boxes. Then, say the words.

1. 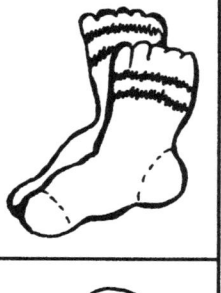 [sock]

2. 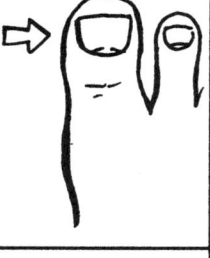 [toe]

3. 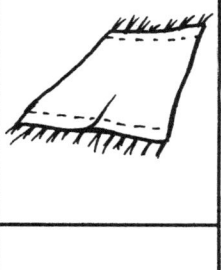 [towel]

4.  [nail]

5. [mitten]

Sounds Abound   119   Copyright © 1993 LinguiSystems, Inc.

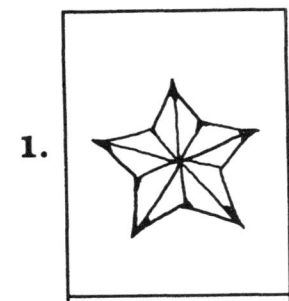

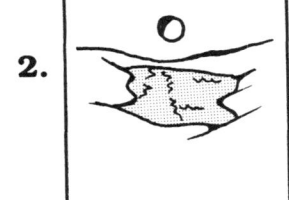

Lots of Words 5

Name_____

Think of as many words as you can that begin with the same sound as the pictures in the boxes. Write the words or draw pictures of the words in the blanks next to the boxes. Then, say the words.

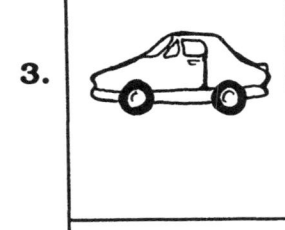

1.
2.
3.
4. 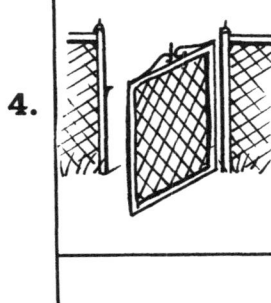
5.

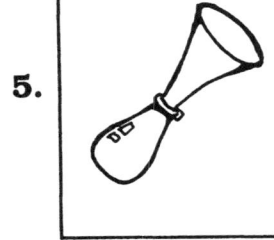

Sounds Abound   120   Copyright © 1993 LinguiSystems, Inc.

Lots of Words 6

Sound Production

Read the words to the child. Then, ask him to tell you as many words as he can that begin with the same sound or sound blend as the word you read.

1. boat
2. dirt
3. fall
4. juice
5. think
6. leaf
7. move
8. new
9. pain
10. run
11. sign
12. take
13. shoot
14. wash
15. chain
16. bed
17. king
18. dig
19. fold
20. gas
21. post
22. tire
23. heart
24. blink
25. breath
26. flew
27. fruit
28. trail
29. steak
30. skin
31. slam
32. smear
33. crib
34. clear
35. great
36. glove
38. speed
37. straw
39. dream
40. plate

The Name Game

Sound Play

Have the children sit in a circle. Ask each child to say her name out loud. Then, have her think of something that begins with the same sound as her first name. Have the children choose words from a specific category, like food. Some examples are given below.

Name	*Category:* *Food*
Evan	egg
Lisa	lemons
Sonya	soup
Tammy	turkey
Karl	cookies
Ben	bananas
Maria	milk

Other possible categories: animals, names of toys, places

Sounds Abound

Go Fish!

Sound Play

Copy pages 123-125. Next, cut out the pictures to make 24 playing cards, enough for two players. Shuffle the cards and deal 5 cards to each player.

Put the remaining cards in a pile. Have the child start the game by asking for a card that begins with the same sound as one of the cards in his hand. If you have a card with the same sound, give it to the child. Have him put the card set beside him. If you don't have a card with the same sound, have the child take a card from the pile. The person with the most cards beside him at the end of the game is the winner.

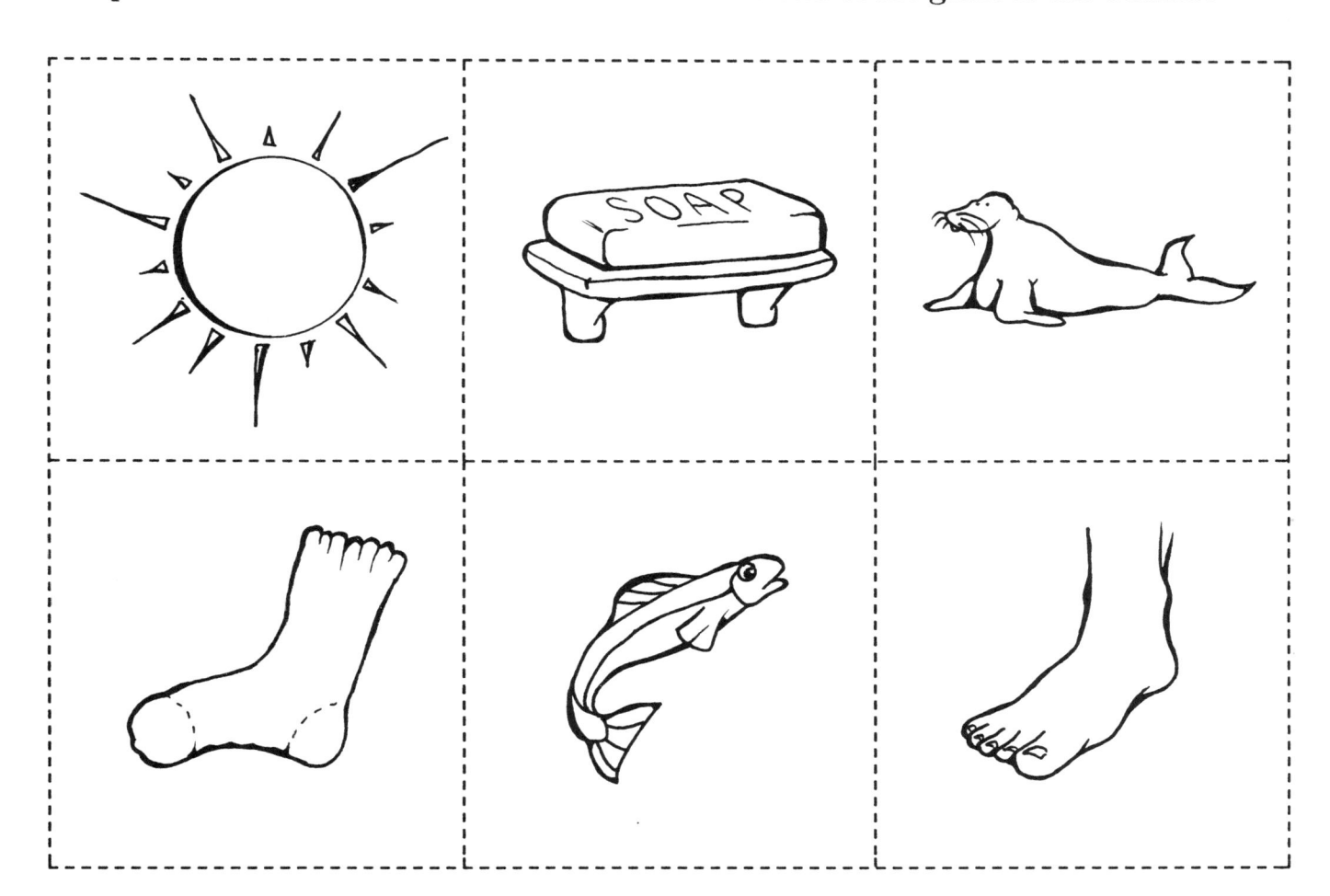

Sounds Abound

Go Fish! continued　　　　　　　　　　　　　　　　　　*Sound Play*

Sounds Abound　　　　　　　　　124　　　　　　　　Copyright © 1993 LinguiSystems, Inc.

Go Fish! *continued* — Sound Play

Sounds Abound
125
Copyright © 1993 LinguiSystems, Inc.

Beginning Sound Song

Sound Play

Have your students look through magazines, sale ads, or old picture books. Next, have them find and cut out pictures of items beginning with a target sound. Have them glue the pictures onto a sheet of construction paper to make a sound collage. Then, use the sound collages to sing the song below together. The song is sung to the tune of "Jimmy Cracked Corn." This activity is adapted from Yopp (1992).

Sing together:

>Who has a /b/ word to share with us?
>
>Who has a /b/ word to share with us?
>
>Who has a /b/ word to share with us?
>
>It must start with a /b/ sound!

Call on volunteers to say one of their words on their sound collages that begins with /b/. Have the child point to the picture as you sing together:

>*Ball* is a word that starts with /b/.
>
>*Ball* is a word that starts with /b/.
>
>*Ball* is a word that starts with /b/.
>
>*Ball* starts with the /b/ sound.

After the children have made several beginning sound collages, review the words with the children. Point to several of the pictures on one of the collages, and have the children guess the beginning sound. Then, sing the song below together to the tune of "Old MacDonald Had a Farm."

>What's the sound that starts these words:
>
>Baby, ball, and bat? (Wait for a response.)
>
>/b/ is the sound that starts these words:
>
>Baby, ball, and bat.
>
>With a /b/, /b/ here and a /b/, /b/ there.
>
>Here a /b/. There a /b/. Everywhere a /b/, /b/.
>
>/b/ is the sound that starts these words:
>
>Baby, ball, and bat!

Beginnings/Endings Pretest *Evaluation*

This pretest uses the Odd One Out format. There are three training items. Use the pictures from pages 96-101 as training items for the child who can't perform correctly on any training items provided. Correct answers should only be given on the training items.

Read each set of words aloud. Then, ask the child to choose the word that doesn't begin or end with the same sound as the other two words.

Training Items

1. bat   bear   king
2. mouse   lake   mom
3. fox   pan   pig

Test Items

Beginning Sounds

1. duck   coat   door
2. moon   mop   leg
3. boat   toe   toy
4. rake   ring   leaf
5. comb   ball   bed
6. lip   milk   lake
7. soap   shot   sock
8. gate   ghost   cow

Ending Sounds

1. duck   sock   nose
2. sun   ball   fan
3. car   hat   gate
4. face   kiss   moon
5. tire   mop   rope
6. dime   thumb   run
7. gas   wash   fish
8. boat   sled   cat

Sounds Abound   Copyright © 1993 LinguiSystems, Inc.

Beginnings/Endings Posttest

Evaluation

This posttest uses the Odd One Out format. There are three training items. Correct answers should only be given on the training items.

Read each set of words aloud. Then, ask the child to choose the word that doesn't begin or end with the same sound as the other two words.

Training Items

1. bees   shell   boy
2. lake   deer   leg
3. rope   pool   pin

Test Items

Beginning Sounds

1. jar   bear   bell
2. run   car   robe
3. door   dish   bone
4. shoe   nose   ship
5. rock   game   girl
6. horn   kite   help
7. map   mom   nail
8. king   coat   girl

Ending Sounds

1. man   egg   sun
2. kite   hat   ring
3. gone   race   house
4. mom   car   some
5. knife   leaf   face
6. soap   zip   rub
7. kiss   wish   push
8. bag   kick   rug

Segmenting and Blending

Segmenting and blending speech sounds is closely related to early reading and writing development. Children who can segment and blend phonemes more easily learn how the alphabet is used for reading and spelling.

Because of the way words are produced, segmenting and blending phonemes can be difficult. Words are spoken with no breaks between individual phonemes. In fact, the sound information about a phoneme is usually spread across several adjacent phonemes. As a result, phonemes are hard to isolate and identify in words. Nevertheless, children need to gain an awareness of phonemes as sound units in order to learn how the alphabet corresponds to the sounds in words.

This section teaches children to segment and blend speech sounds. Activities begin with segmenting and blending syllables. Syllables in words are much easier to identify and manipulate than are phonemes. Thus, the syllable level activities can help children learn the segmental nature of speech.

Once children have become familiar with segmenting and blending syllables, the same activities are used to teach the segmenting and blending of phonemes. Some children will grasp the segmental nature of speech faster than others. For those children, you should move directly to segmenting and blending phonemes without completing the syllable activities.

Segmenting Syllables

In this section, children will learn to segment and blend the syllables of words. Pictures representing one-, two-, and three-syllable words are found on pages 132-139. The number of squares under each picture corresponds to each syllable in the word. Use the *say-it-and-move-it* procedure (Ball & Blachman, 1988) outlined below to draw the children's attention to the syllables in words. Use coins or chips as tokens when completing the segmentation activities.

1. Put the same number of tokens as there are squares on the picture.

2. Have children say each syllable of the word separately while moving a token into the corresponding square.

3. After the children say each syllable of a multisyllabic word and move the tokens into the squares, have them blend the syllables together and say the whole word.

For additional practice in segmenting and blending syllables, use the lists of one-, two-, and three-syllable words on pages 140-141, tokens, and the activity sheet on page 142. A variation of the *say-it-and-move-it* procedure can be used as follows.

1. Have the children place three tokens above the line on page 142.

2. Read aloud a word from one of the lists.

3. Have the children say each of the syllables in the word separately while moving a token into a square below the line.

4. After the children say each syllable of a multisyllabic word and move the tokens into the squares, have them blend the syllables together and say the whole word.

The final task in this section gives children more practice segmenting syllables. They'll learn to segment and delete the initial or final sylla-ables from two-syllable words.

Segmenting

Segmenting Syllables

Here is a list of words to refer to when completing the activities on pages 132-139.

Segmenting 1, page 132	*Segmenting 5, page 136*
cowboy	rabbit
rainbow	tornado
football	snow
airplane	spaghetti

Segmenting 2, page 133	*Segmenting 6, page 137*
balloon	carrot
ball	elephant
banana	tomato
pumpkin	snake

Segmenting 3, page 134	*Segmenting 7, page 138*
moon	gorilla
telephone	flower
earring	finger
potato	computer

Segmenting 4, page 135	*Segmenting 8, page 139*
hamburger	kite
hose	bacon
pencil	octopus
Popsicle	pickle

Segmenting 1   Name _____

Look at the pictures. Each word pictured has the same number of syllables as the number of squares under it. As you say each syllable, move a token into a square under the picture. Then, blend the syllables together and say the whole word.

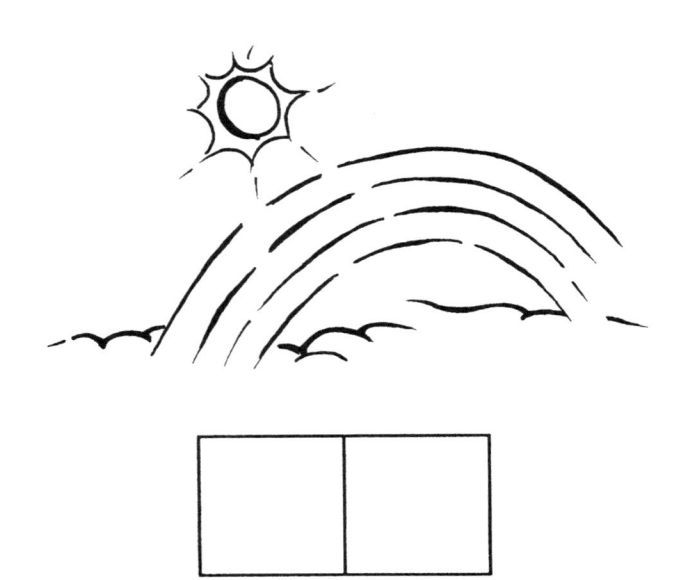

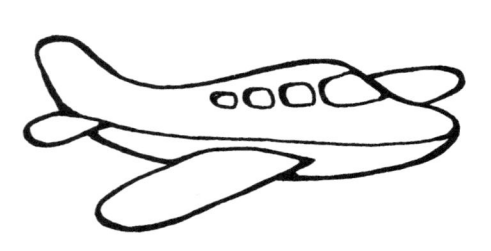

Sounds Abound   Copyright © 1993 LinguiSystems, Inc.

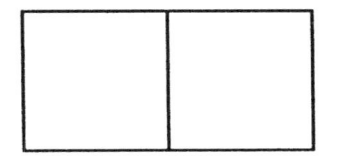

Segmenting 2

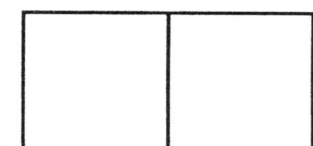

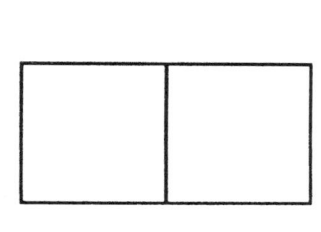

Name _____

Look at the pictures. Each word pictured has the same number of syllables as the number of squares under it. As you say each syllable, move a token into a square under the picture. Then, blend the syllables together and say the whole word.

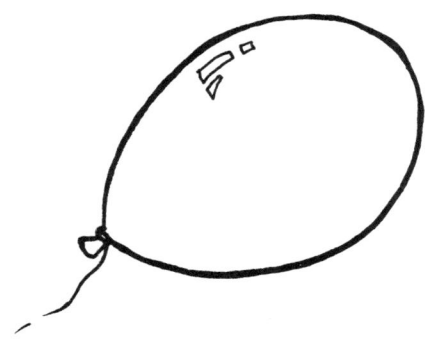

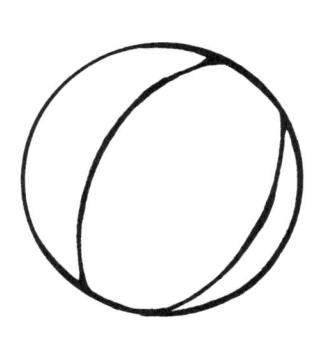

Sounds Abound

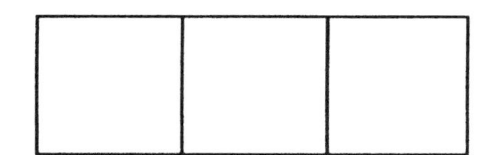

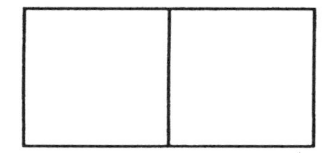

Copyright © 1993 LinguiSystems, Inc.

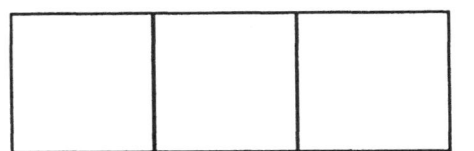

Segmenting 3 Name _____

Look at the pictures. Each word pictured has the same number of syllables as the number of squares under it. As you say each syllable, move a token into a square under the picture. Then, blend the syllables together and say the whole word.

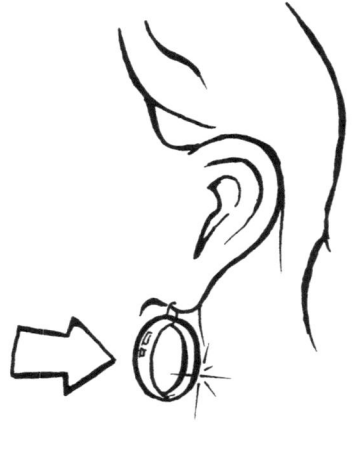

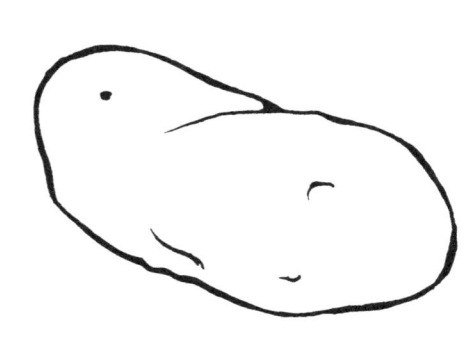

Sounds Abound   134   Copyright © 1993 LinguiSystems, Inc.

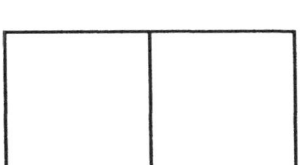

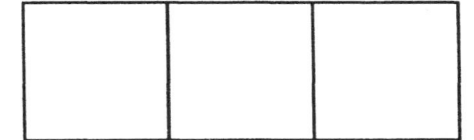

Segmenting 4   Name _____

Look at the pictures. Each word pictured has the same number of syllables as the number of squares under it. As you say each syllable, move a token into a square under the picture. Then, blend the syllables together and say the whole word.

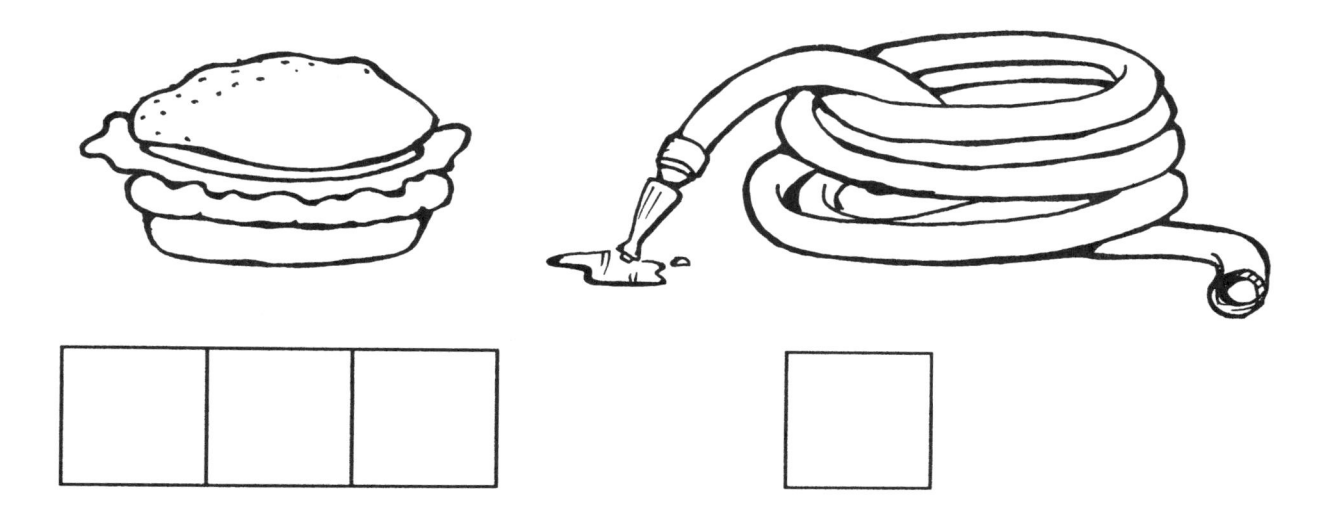

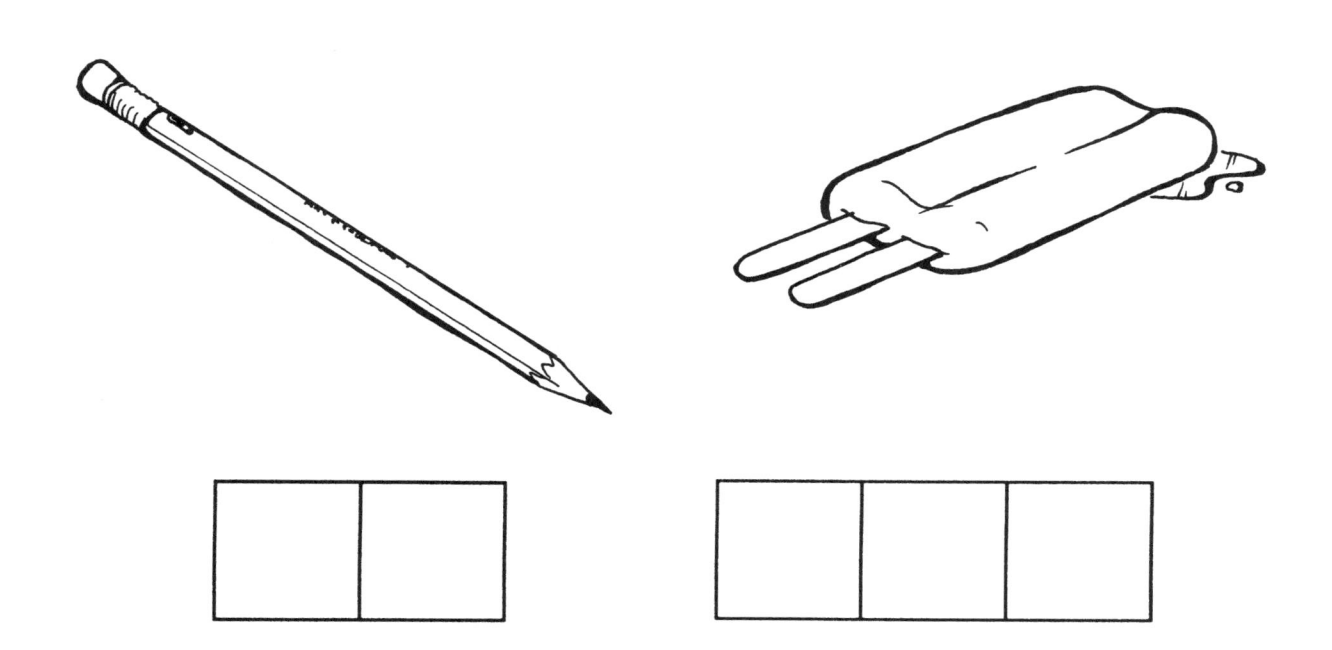

Sounds Abound   135   Copyright © 1993 LinguiSystems, Inc.

Segmenting 5   Name _____

Look at the pictures. Each word pictured has the same number of syllables as the number of squares under it. As you say each syllable, move a token into a square under the picture. Then, blend the syllables together and say the whole word.

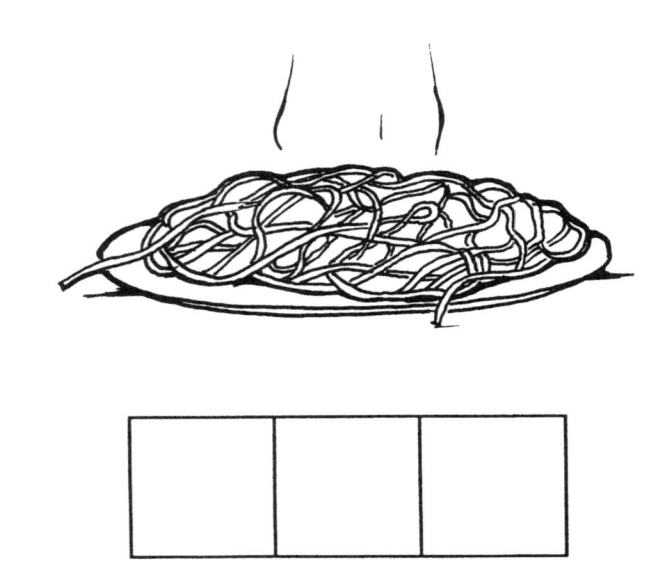

Sounds Abound   136   Copyright © 1993 LinguiSystems, Inc.

Segmenting 6   Name _____

Look at the pictures. Each word pictured has the same number of syllables as the number of squares under it. As you say each syllable, move a token into a square under the picture. Then, blend the syllables together and say the whole word.

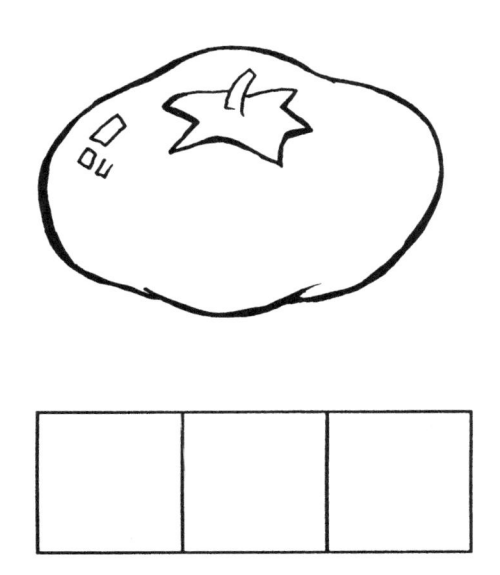

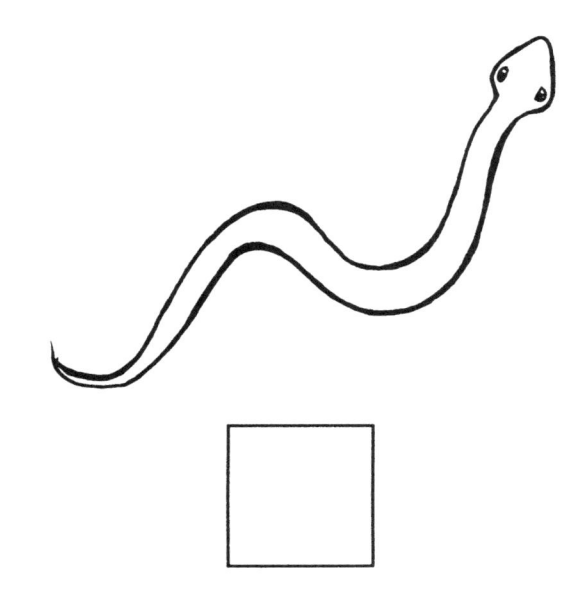

Sounds Abound

Segmenting 7   Name _____

Look at the pictures. Each word pictured has the same number of syllables as the number of squares under it. As you say each syllable, move a token into a square under the picture. Then, blend the syllables together and say the whole word.

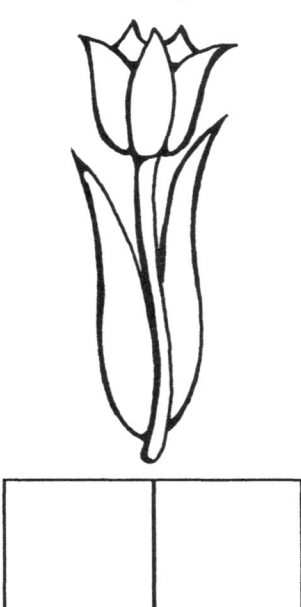

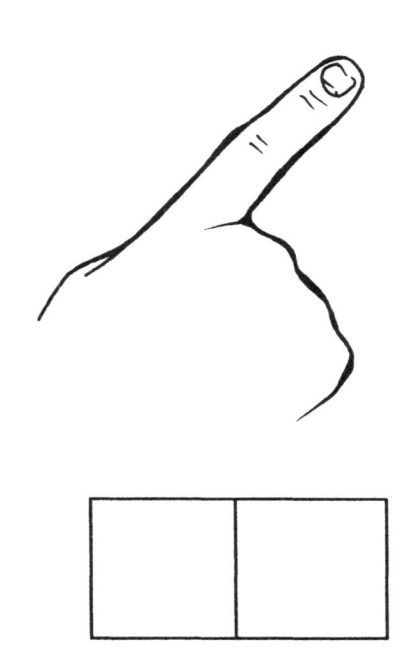

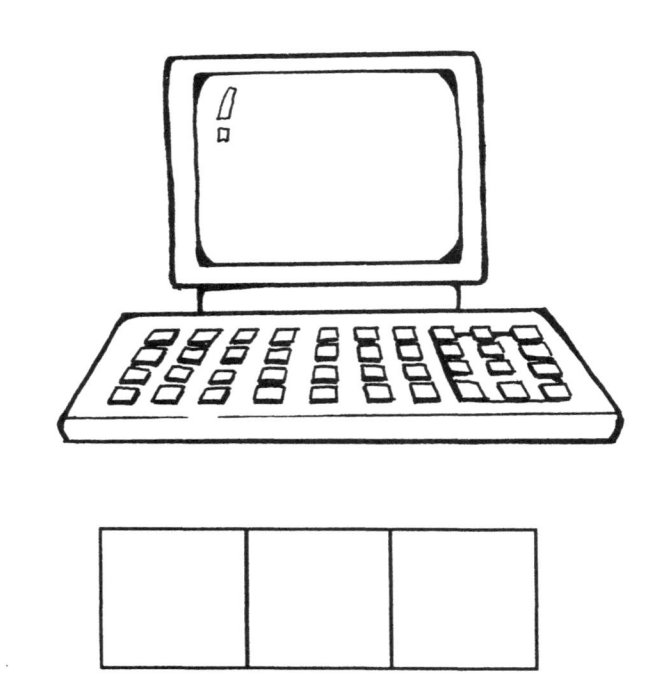

Sounds Abound   138   Copyright © 1993 LinguiSystems, Inc.

Segmenting 8

Name _____

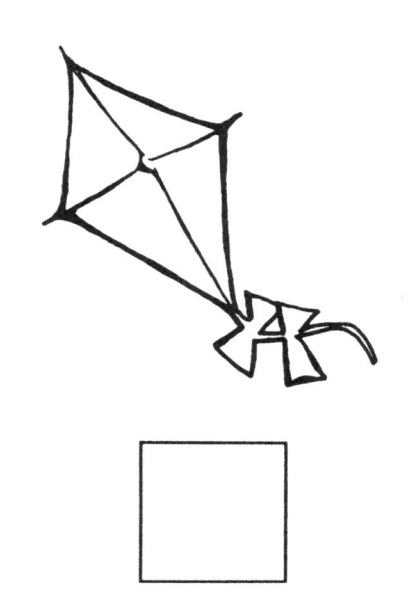

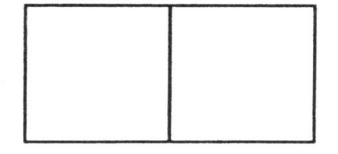

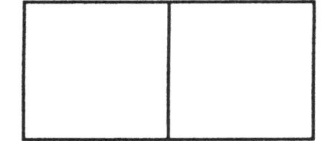

Look at the pictures. Each word pictured has the same number of syllables as the number of squares under it. As you say each syllable, move a token into a square under the picture. Then, blend the syllables together and say the whole word.

Sounds Abound   139   Copyright © 1993 LinguiSystems, Inc.

Segmenting 9

Segmenting Syllables

One-, two-, and three- syllable words are listed below. Use them with page 142. Read each word aloud. Next, have the child say each syllable of the word separately while he moves a token into the corresponding square. Then, have the child blend the syllables together and say the whole word.

1. mom (1)
2. animal (3)
3. playground (2)
4. basketball (3)
5. bird (1)
6. teacher (2)
7. pajamas (3)
8. kitty (2)
9. monster (2)
10. toy (1)
11. vacation (3)
12. party (2)
13. understand (3)
14. tree (1)
15. happy (2)
16. remember (3)
17. tricycle (3)
18. music (2)
19. school (1)
20. present (2)

21. screwdriver (3)
22. tiger (2)
23. Saturday (3)
24. girl (1)
25. dessert (2)
26. astronaut (3)
27. another (3)
28. mother (2)
29. frog (1)
30. ambulance (3)
31. Snoopy (2)
32. cucumber (3)
33. bath (1)
34. mosquito (3)
35. December (3)
36. police (2)
37. mouth (1)
38. summer (2)
39. whisper (2)
40. sky (1)

Segmenting 10

Segmenting Syllables

One-, two-, and three- syllable words are listed below. Use them with page 142. Read each word aloud. Next, have the child say each syllable of the word separately while she moves a token into the corresponding square. Then, have the child blend the syllables together and say the whole word.

1. carnival (3)
2. mountain (2)
3. tummy (2)
4. important (3)
5. game (1)
6. raisin (2)
7. October (3)
8. thunder (2)
9. coffee (2)
10. house (1)
11. Dracula (3)
12. crazy (2)
13. typewriter (3)
14. brown (1)
15. weekend (2)
16. principal (3)
17. jungle (2)
18. me (1)
19. somersault (3)
20. dish (1)
21. overhead (3)
22. puppy (2)
23. rug (1)
24. magnify (3)
25. purple (2)
26. piano (3)
27. horse (1)
28. cinnamon (3)
29. booklet (2)
30. yesterday (3)
31. boat (1)
32. elbow (2)
33. spaghetti (3)
34. letter (2)
35. fly (1)
36. exercise (3)
37. pocket (2)
38. cup (1)
39. radio (3)
40. simple (2)

segmenting 11 *Segmenting Syllables*

Use this activity sheet with pages 140-141. Put three tokens above the line. Have the child say each syllable of a word as she moves a token into a square. Then, have the child blend the syllables together and say the whole word.

Sounds Abound   Copyright © 1993 LinguiSystems, Inc

What's Left? 1   Name _____

In the *What's Left?* activities, the child will learn to divide words into syllables. In these activities, have the child say the word that remains after deleting the first or last syllable.

Use this page for training. For the first item, point to the cup and the cake and say *cupcake*. Then, have the child say *cupcake*. Next, cover the picture of the cup and ask her to say *cupcake* without saying *cup*. Do the same for the *toothbrush* and *doorbell*.

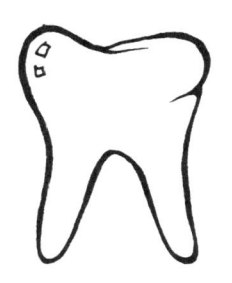

Sounds Abound   143   Copyright © 1993 LinguiSystems, Inc.

What's Left? 2

Deleting Syllables (initial)

Read each word aloud. Then, have the child say the word that remains after deleting the first syllable. For example, in the first item, say the word *railroad*. Then, ask the child to say *railroad* without saying *rail*.

1. <u>rail</u>road
2. <u>bath</u>tub
3. <u>pea</u>nut
4. <u>base</u>ball
5. <u>Sun</u>day
6. <u>side</u>walk
7. <u>back</u>yard
8. <u>he</u>ro
9. <u>sur</u>prise
10. <u>en</u>tire
11. <u>gui</u>tar
12. <u>mo</u>tel
13. <u>ba</u>by
14. <u>re</u>fresh
15. <u>a</u>long
16. <u>be</u>side
17. <u>ad</u>dress
18. <u>chim</u>ney
19. <u>be</u>lief
20. <u>a</u>corn
21. <u>rab</u>bit
22. <u>mil</u>ky
23. <u>re</u>turn
24. <u>per</u>son
25. <u>tar</u>get
26. <u>en</u>joy
27. <u>be</u>low
28. <u>a</u>ware
29. <u>mis</u>take
30. <u>val</u>ue
31. <u>ba</u>sic
32. <u>a</u>board
33. <u>fab</u>ric
34. <u>gar</u>lic
35. <u>cur</u>few
36. <u>re</u>gard
37. <u>ca</u>ble
38. <u>ham</u>ster
39. <u>Ja</u>pan
40. <u>Pep</u>si

Sounds Abound

Copyright © 1993 LinguiSystems, Inc.

What's Left? 3

Deleting Syllables (final)

Read each word aloud. Then, have the child say the word that remains after deleting the last syllable. For example, in the first item, say the word *bedroom*. Then, ask the child to say *bedroom* without saying *room*.

1. bed<u>room</u>
2. play<u>ground</u>
3. pan<u>cake</u>
4. sun<u>set</u>
5. hand<u>cuff</u>
6. out<u>side</u>
7. ro<u>bot</u>
8. car<u>toon</u>
9. win<u>ter</u>
10. ri<u>der</u>
11. book<u>let</u>
12. mi<u>nus</u>
13. fun<u>nel</u>
14. pen<u>cil</u>
15. sher<u>iff</u>
16. safe<u>ty</u>
17. fan<u>cy</u>
18. can<u>dy</u>
19. win<u>dow</u>
20. wal<u>nut</u>
21. neck<u>lace</u>
22. light<u>ning</u>
23. slip<u>per</u>
24. bat<u>ter</u>
25. pi<u>rate</u>
26. stir<u>rup</u>
27. su<u>per</u>
28. ti<u>ger</u>
29. nee<u>dle</u>
30. gra<u>vy</u>
31. ber<u>ry</u>
32. brown<u>ie</u>
33. bar<u>ber</u>
34. cher<u>ish</u>
35. let<u>tuce</u>
36. laugh<u>ter</u>
37. dol<u>lar</u>
38. sand<u>wich</u>
39. ten<u>nis</u>
40. cap<u>tain</u>

Sounds Abound

Blending Syllables

The *say-it-and-move-it* procedure used in Segmenting Syllables gives some practice in blending syllables. This section provides additional materials for blending syllables. On pages 147-151, pictures representing two- and three-syllable words are shown.

Copy each of the following pages and cut the pictures into two or three pieces along the dotted lines. Show the children each piece of a picture separately. Next, say the corresponding syllable. Then, have the children move the pieces together as they blend the syllables and say the whole word.

Blending   1   Name _____

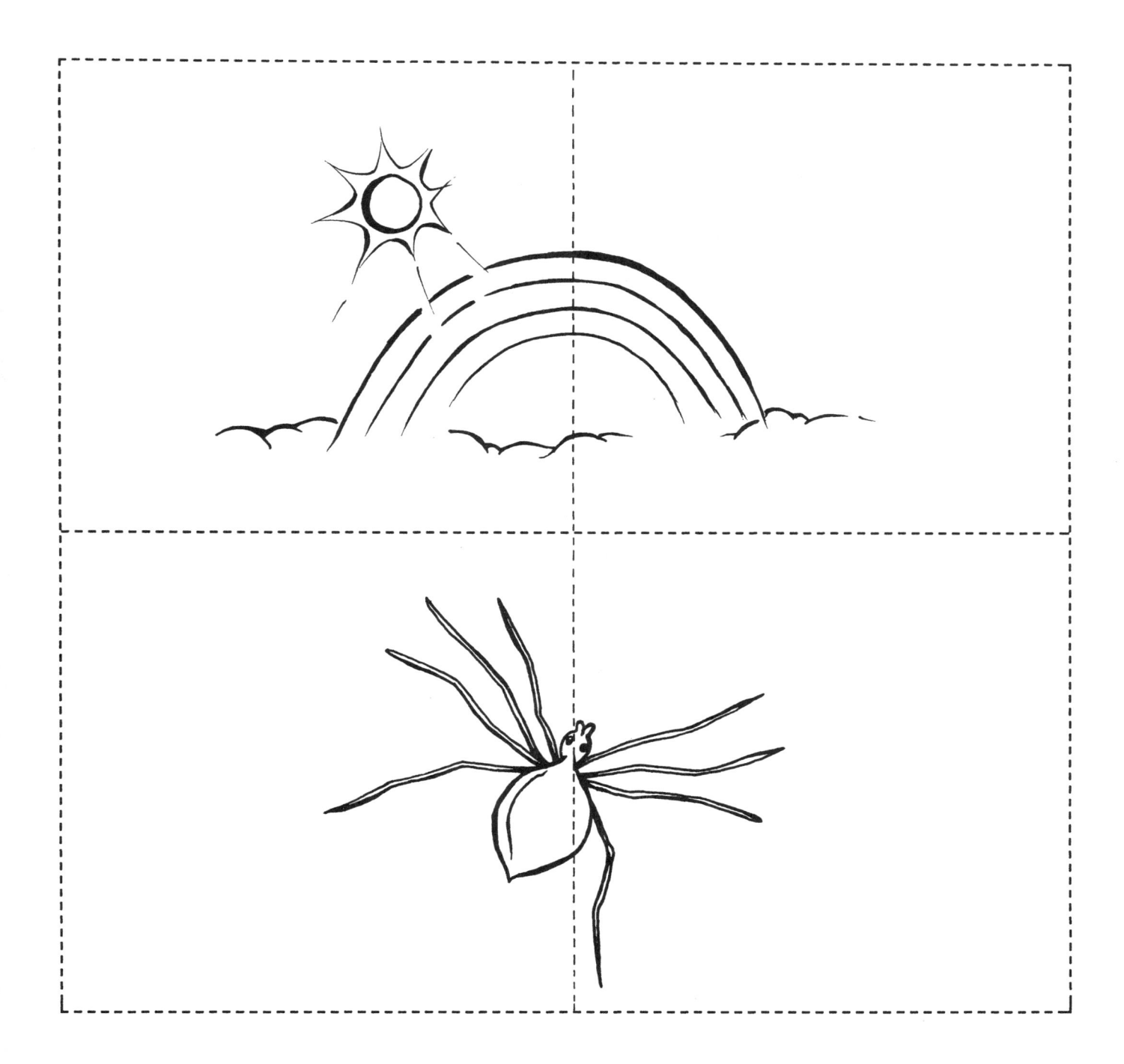

Use these pictures to help you blend syllables.

Sounds Abound   147   Copyright © 1993 LinguiSystems, Inc.

Blending 2   Name _____

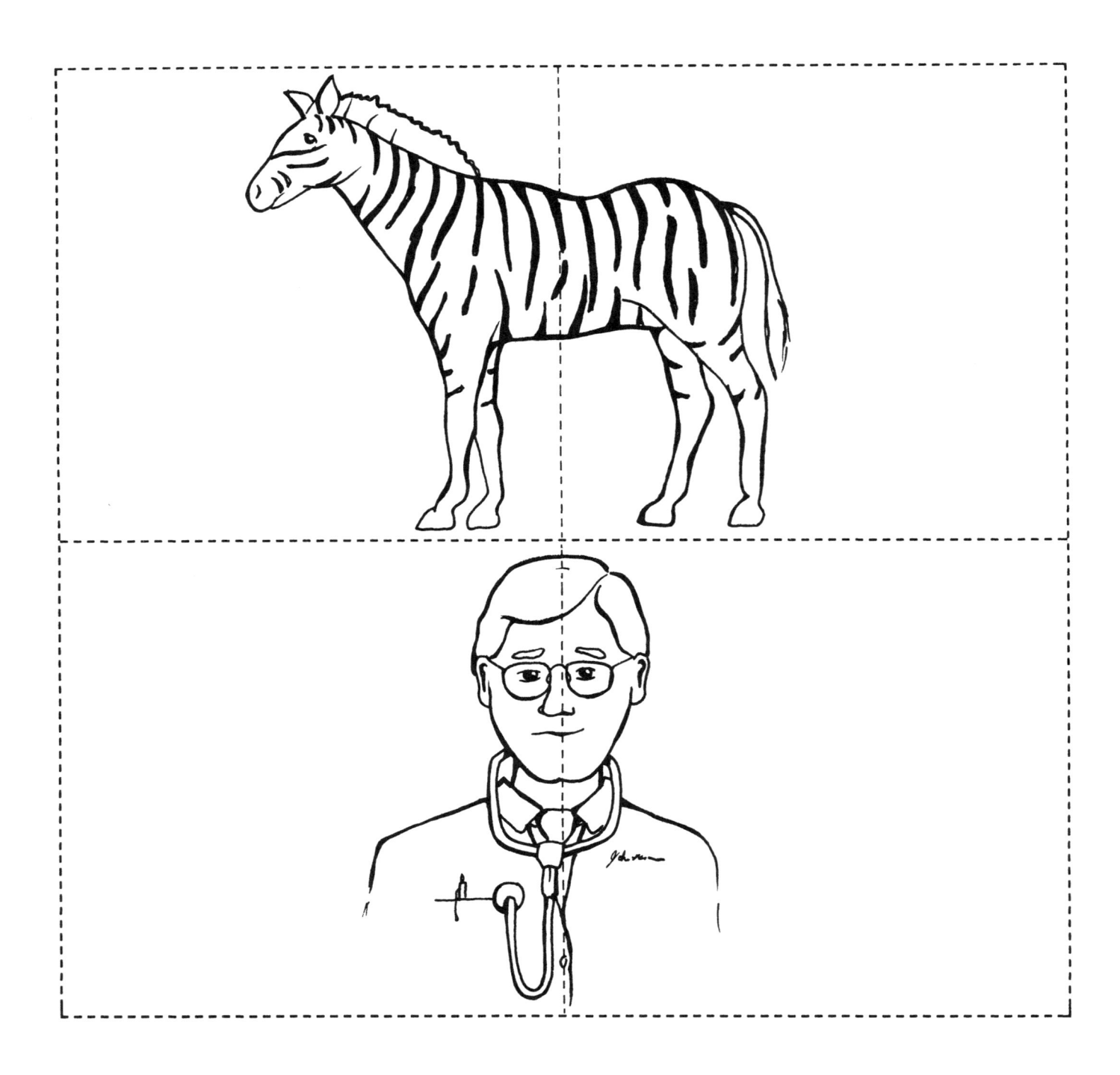

Use these pictures to help you blend syllables.

Sounds Abound   148   Copyright © 1993 LinguiSystems, Inc.

Blending

3   Name _____

Use these pictures to help you blend syllables.

Sounds Abound   149   Copyright © 1993 LinguiSystems, Inc.

Blending 4   Name _____

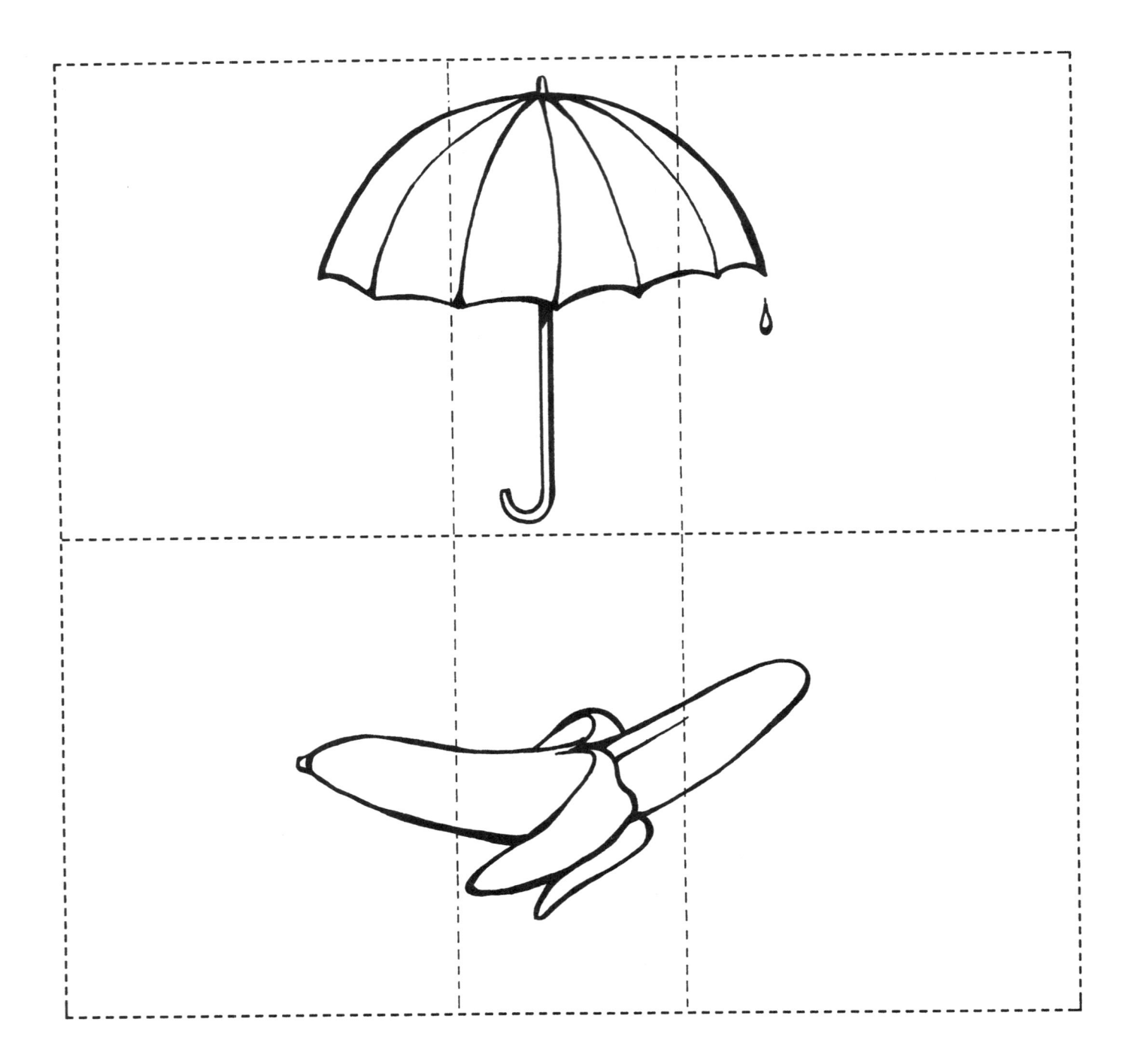

Use these pictures to help you blend syllables.

Sounds Abound   150   Copyright © 1993 LinguiSystems, Inc

Blending

5   Name _____

Use these pictures to help you blend syllables.

Sounds Abound   151   Copyright © 1993 LinguiSystems, Inc.

Blending   6   *Blending Syllables*

Read each word aloud to the child, one syllable at a time. Then, have the child blend the syllables together. You may want to use a hand puppet for this task. Tell the child that the puppet talks differently because he says only one syllable at a time. Ask the child to listen carefully to the puppet and then say the words the right way.

1. pillow
2. animal
3. hospital
4. also
5. strawberry
6. behind
7. children
8. beautiful
9. helicopter
10. almost
11. important
12. father
13. alligator
14. difficult
15. river
16. picture
17. together
18. kindergarten
19. summer
20. Washington

21. president
22. mother
23. understand
24. often
25. happy
26. afternoon
27. jungle
28. monster
29. photograph
30. macaroni
31. yesterday
32. music
33. secretary
34. wiggle
35. triangle
36. department
37. ocean
38. grasshopper
39. butterfly
40. lemonade

Sounds Abound   Copyright © 1993 LinguiSystems, Inc.

Segmenting Phonemes

In this section, children will learn to divide words into phonemes. Pictures of words containing two or three phonemes are on pages 155-158. The number of squares under each picture corresponds to each phoneme in the word. To complete the activities, use the *say-it-and-move-it* procedure (Ball & Blachman, 1988) outlined below. To help the children isolate phonemes, target words contain mostly continuant sounds, like fricatives, vowels, liquids, and affricates. In some instances, words containing final stop consonants are used.

1. Put the same number of tokens as there are squares on the picture.

2. Have the children say each phoneme in the word while moving a token into the corresponding square below the line.

3. After the children say each phoneme and move the tokens into the squares, have them blend the phonemes together and say the whole word.

For additional practice in segmenting phonemes, use the lists of words containing one, two, three, or four phonemes on pages 159 and 161, tokens, and the activity sheets on pages 160 and 162. A variation of the *say-it-and-move-it* procedure can be used as follows.

1. Have the children place three or four tokens above the line on page 160 or 162.

2. Read aloud a word from one of the lists.

3. Have the children say each phoneme in the word while moving a token into the corresponding square below the line.

4. After the children say each phoneme and move the tokens into the squares, have them blend the phonemes together and say the whole word.

The final task in this section gives children more practice segmenting phonemes. They'll learn to segment and delete the initial or final phonemes and say the words that remain.

Sounds Abound

Segmenting

Segmenting Phonemes

Here is a list of words to refer to when completing the activities on pages 155-158.

Segmenting 1, page 155

shoe

zoo

fish

face

Segmenting 2, page 156

sew

leaf

cheese

five

Segmenting 3, page 157

knee

nose

feet

lake

Segmenting 4, page 158

eight

soup

fan

nut

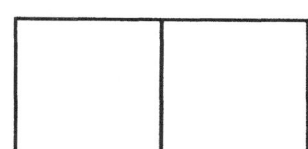

Segmenting 1

Name _____

Look at the pictures. Each word pictured has the same number of sounds as the number of squares under it. As you say each sound, move a token into a square under the picture. Then, blend the sounds together and say the whole word.

Sounds Abound 155 Copyright © 1993 LinguiSystems, Inc.

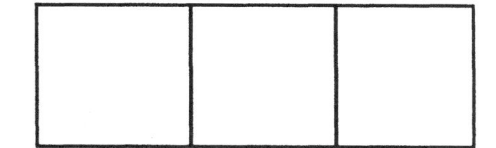

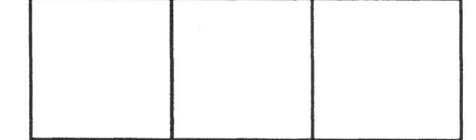

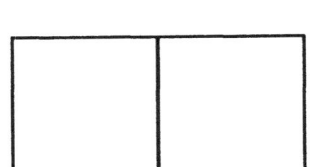

Segmenting 2

Name _____

Look at the pictures. Each word pictured has the same number of sounds as the number of squares under it. As you say each sound, move a token into a square under the picture. Then, blend the sounds together and say the whole word.

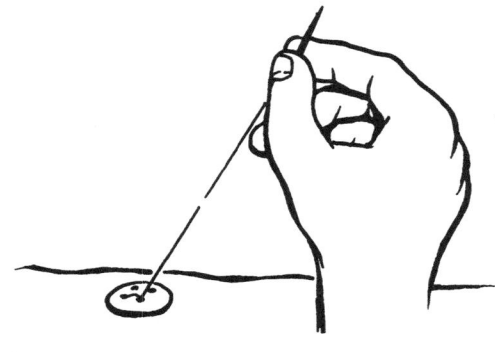

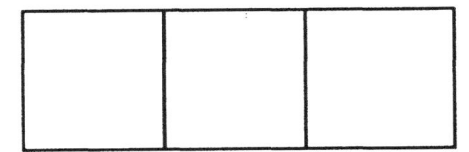

Sounds Abound   156   Copyright © 1993 LinguiSystems, Inc.

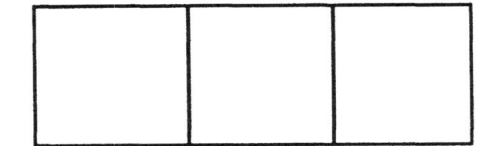

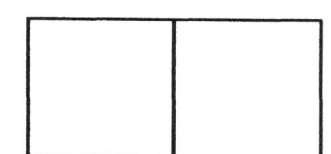

Segmenting 3

Name _____

Look at the pictures. Each word pictured has the same number of sounds as the number of squares under it. As you say each sound, move a token into a square under the picture. Then, blend the sounds together and say the whole word.

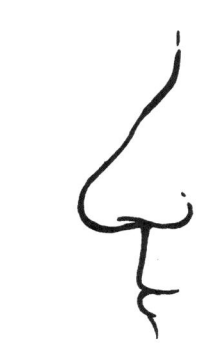

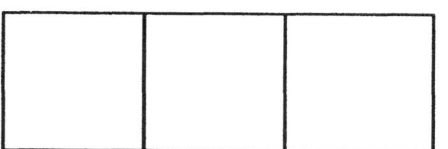

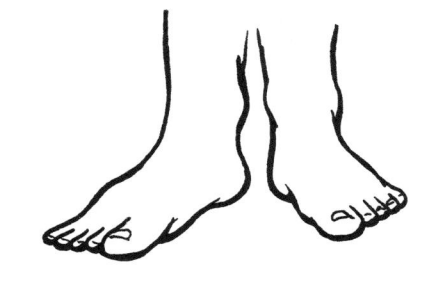

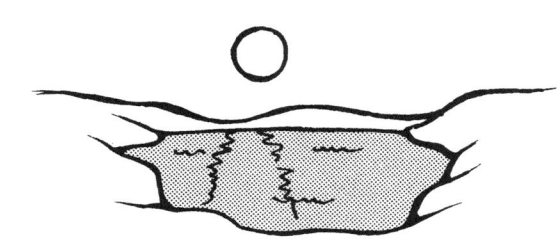

Sounds Abound 157 Copyright © 1993 LinguiSystems, Inc.

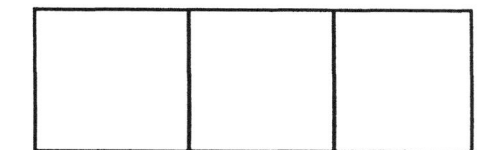

segmenting 4   Name _____

Look at the pictures. Each word pictured has the same number of sounds as the number of squares under it. As you say each sound, move a token into a square under the picture. Then, blend the sounds together and say the whole word.

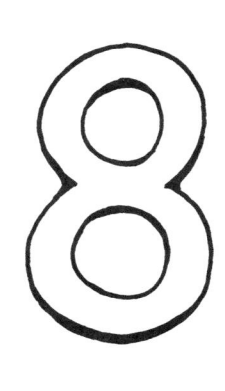

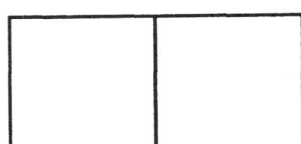

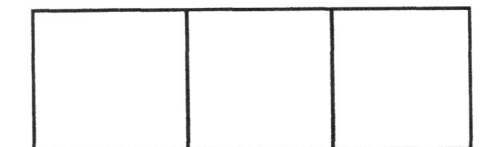

Sounds Abound

Segmenting 5

Segmenting Phonemes

Use this word list with page 160. Read each word aloud. Next, have the child say each phoneme of the word separately while he moves a token into each of the corresponding squares below the line. Then, have the child blend the phonemes together and say the whole word.

1. she	ex. sh e	21. up	
2. say		22. love	
3. size		23. sigh	
4. each		24. ah	
5. shave		25. live	
6. I		26. mop	
7. me		27. may	
8. of		28. in	
9. laugh		29. miss	
10. oh		30. shoot	
11. off		31. odd	
12. sit		32. sssss	
13. sheet		33. like	
14. age		34. nice	
15. nice		35. new	
16. shhhh		36. net	
17. chose		37. mouth	
18. joy		38. oat	
19. race		39. shop	
20. rock		40. night	

Sounds Abound

Segmenting 6

Segmenting Phonemes

Use this activity sheet with the word list on page 159. Put three tokens above the line. Have the child say each phoneme as she moves a token into a square. Then, have the child blend the phonemes together and say the whole word.

Sounds Abound   Copyright © 1993 LinguiSystems, Inc.

Segmenting 7

Segmenting Phonemes (difficult)

This activity is more difficult than the previous phoneme segmentation activity because it contains words with consonant clusters.

Use this word list with page 162. Read each word aloud. Next, have the child say each phoneme of the word separately while he moves a token into each of the corresponding squares below the line. Then, have the child blend the phonemes together and say the word.

1. snow   ex. s n ow
2. pro
3. free
4. crow
5. fry
6. clay
7. ski
8. play
9. slow
10. stay

11. fox
12. flat
13. best
14. wasp
15. disk
16. plate
17. nest
18. cats
19. stop
20. dump

segmenting 8

Segmenting Phonemes

Use this activity sheet with the word list on page 161. Put four tokens above the line. Have the child say each phoneme as he moves a token into a square. Then, have the child blend the phonemes together and say the whole word.

What's Left? 1

Deleting Phonemes (initial)

The phoneme deletion task can be used to teach the child to divide words into phonemes. Read each word aloud. Then, have the child say the word that remains after deleting the first sound. For example, for the first item, say *fall*. Then, ask the child to say *fall* without saying *fff*. Be sure to say the first sound and not the letter name.

1. fall
2. sheet
3. send
4. farm
5. sit
6. land
7. rice
8. lie
9. chair
10. toy
11. mask
12. near
13. tape
14. Kim
15. page
16. learn
17. sand
18. cold
19. tar
20. pink

21. sour
22. feet
23. shelf
24. rich
25. shin
26. mat
27. sold
28. shout
29. chart
30. few
31. slow
32. throw
33. shrug
34. plate
35. sleeve
36. thread
37. blast
38. play
39. smile
40. shrub

What's Left? 2

Deleting Phonemes (final)

Read each word aloud. Then, have the child say the word that remains after deleting the final sound. For example, for the first item, say *nose*. Then, ask the child to say *nose* without saying *zzz*. Be sure to say the last sound and not the letter name.

1. nose
2. save
3. niece
4. life
5. mice
6. couch
7. page
8. beach
9. force
10. seat
11. grape
12. team
13. bone
14. mean
15. rice
16. pave
17. life
18. bike
19. make
20. pipe
21. group
22. boat
23. soup
24. beef
25. dice
26. treat
27. soak
28. rose
29. neat
30. farm
31. teach
32. scorn
33. cart
34. bust
35. lamp
36. paint
37. heard
38. grasp
39. belt
40. build

Sounds Abound

Copyright © 1993 LinguiSystems, Inc.

Blending Phonemes

The *say-it-and-move-it* procedure used in Segmenting Phonemes gives some practice in blending phonemes. This section provides additional materials for blending phonemes. On pages 166-173, pictures representing two- and three-phoneme words are shown.

Copy each of the following pages and cut the pictures into two or three pieces along the dotted lines. Show the children each piece of a picture separately. Next, say the corresponding phoneme. Then, have the children move the pieces together as they blend the syllables and say the whole word.

Blending

1

Blending Phonemes

Use these pictures to help the child blend phonemes.

Sounds Abound — 166 — Copyright © 1993 LinguiSystems, Inc.

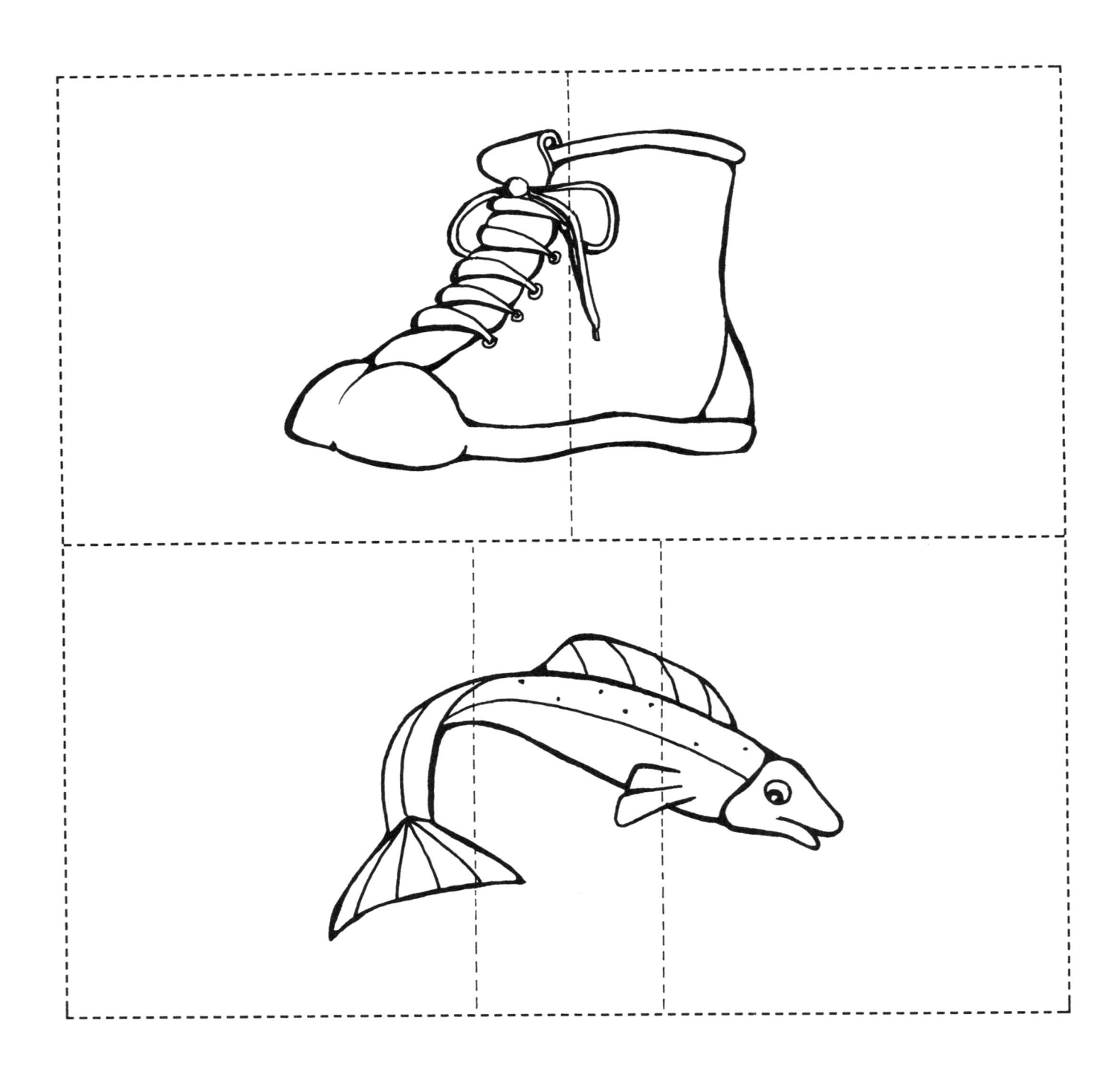

Blending

2

Blending Phonemes

Use these pictures to help the child blend phonemes.

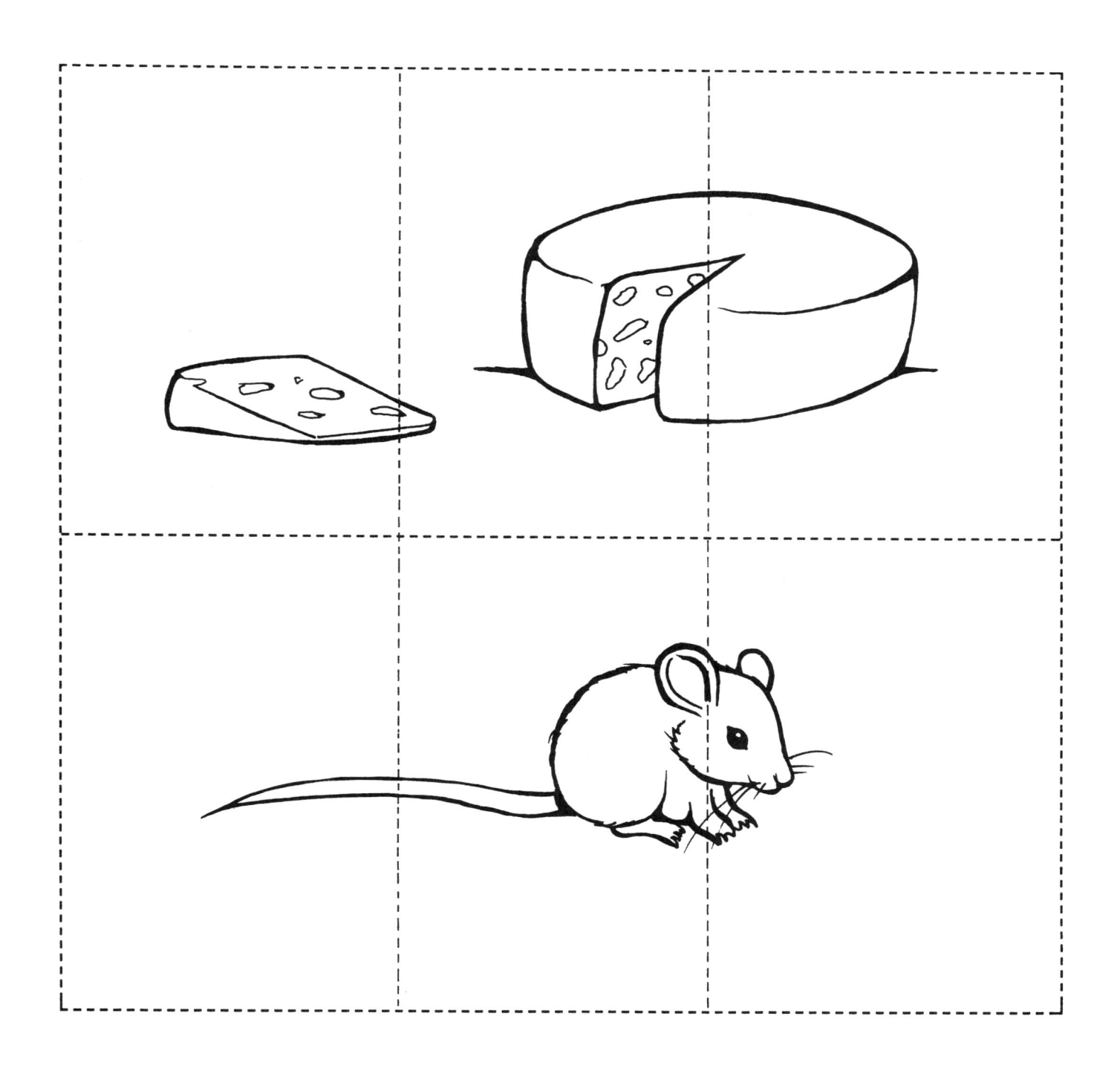

Blending

3

Blending Phonemes

Use these pictures to help the child blend phonemes.

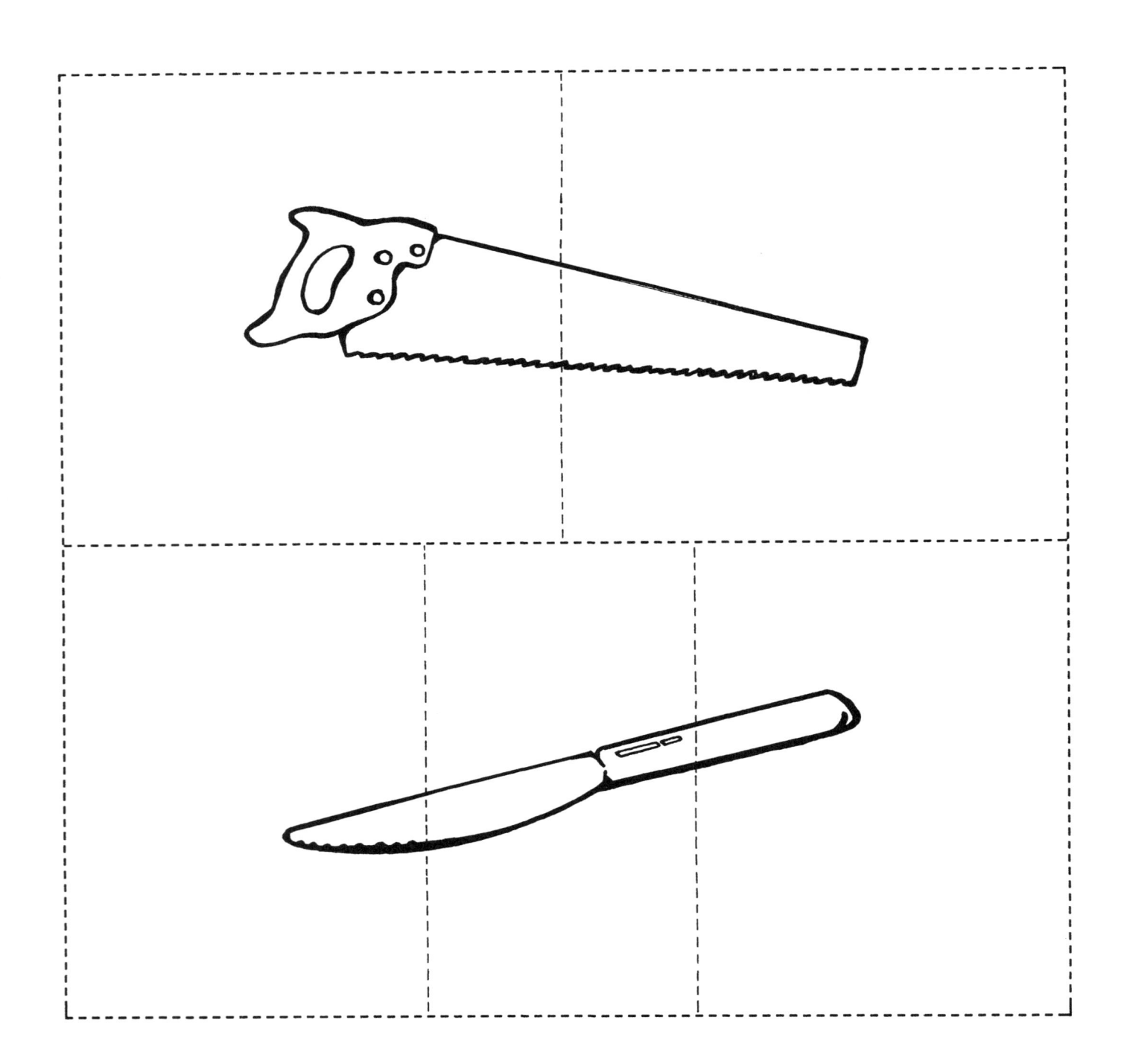

Blending

4

Blending Phonemes

Use these pictures to help the child blend phonemes.

Sounds Abound — 169 — Copyright © 1993 LinguiSystems, Inc.

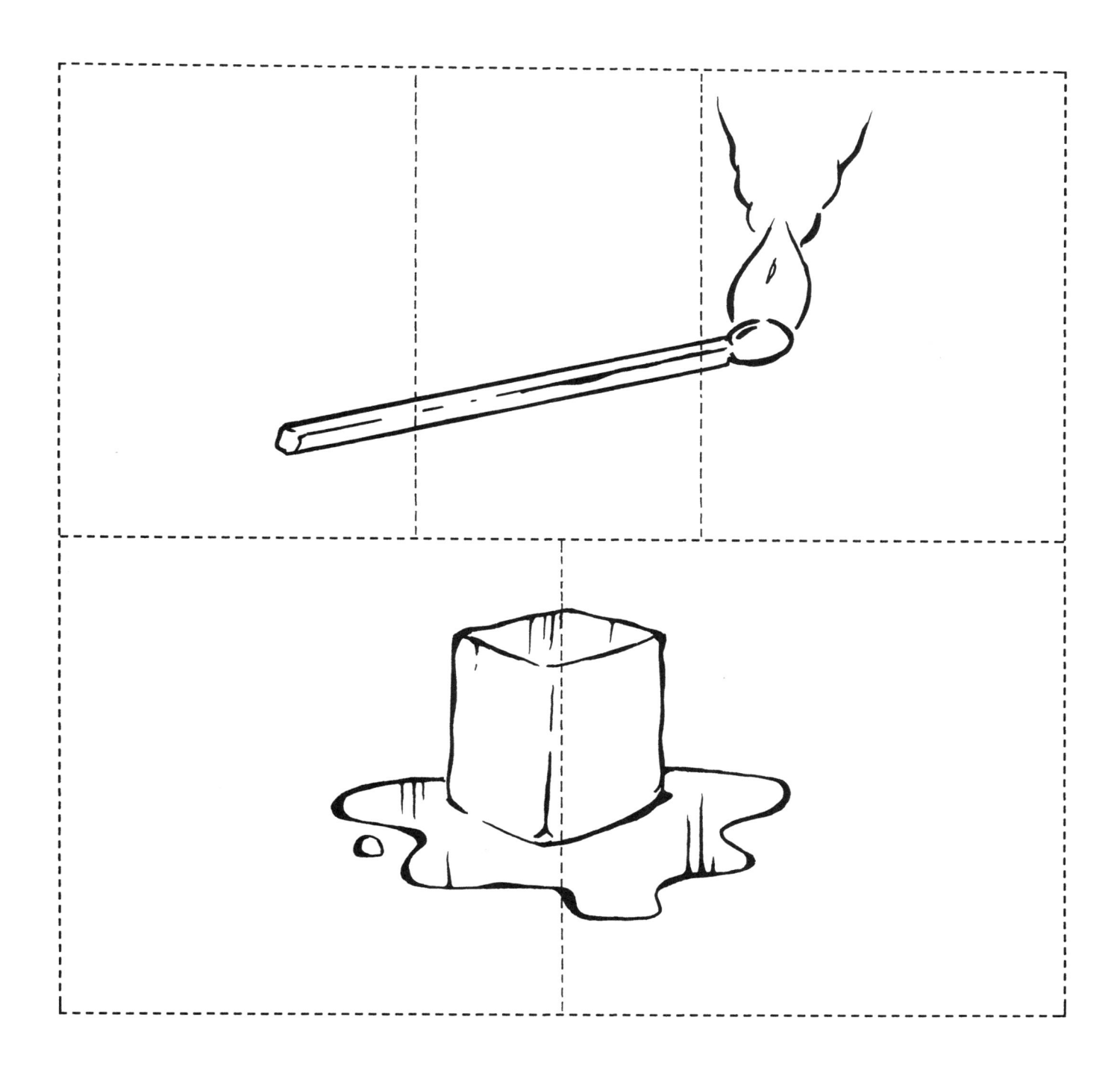

Blending 5 *Blending Phonemes*

Use these pictures to help the child blend phonemes.

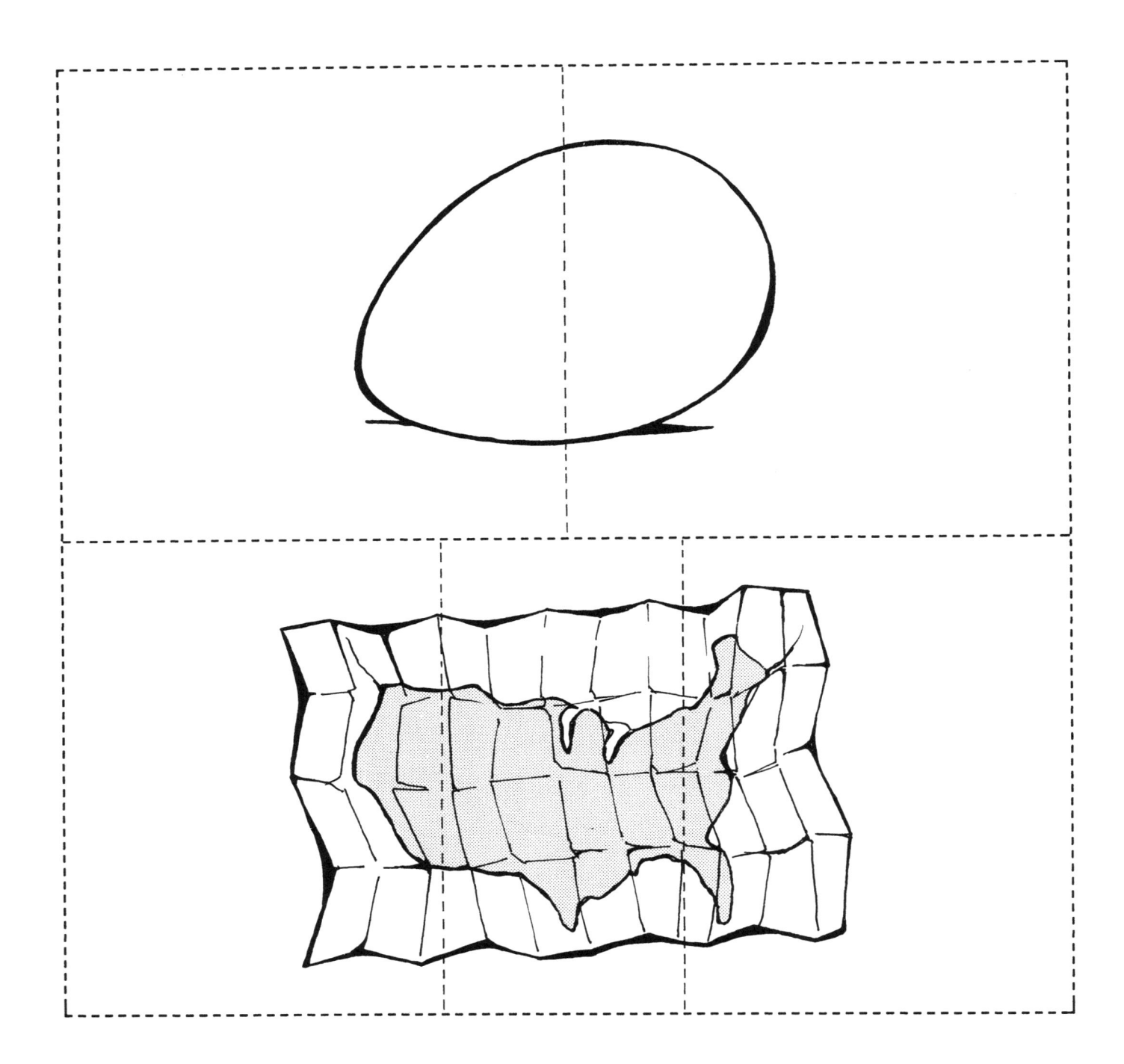

Blending 6 *Blending Phonemes*

Use these pictures to help the child blend phonemes.

Sounds Abound — 171 — Copyright © 1993 LinguiSystems, Inc.

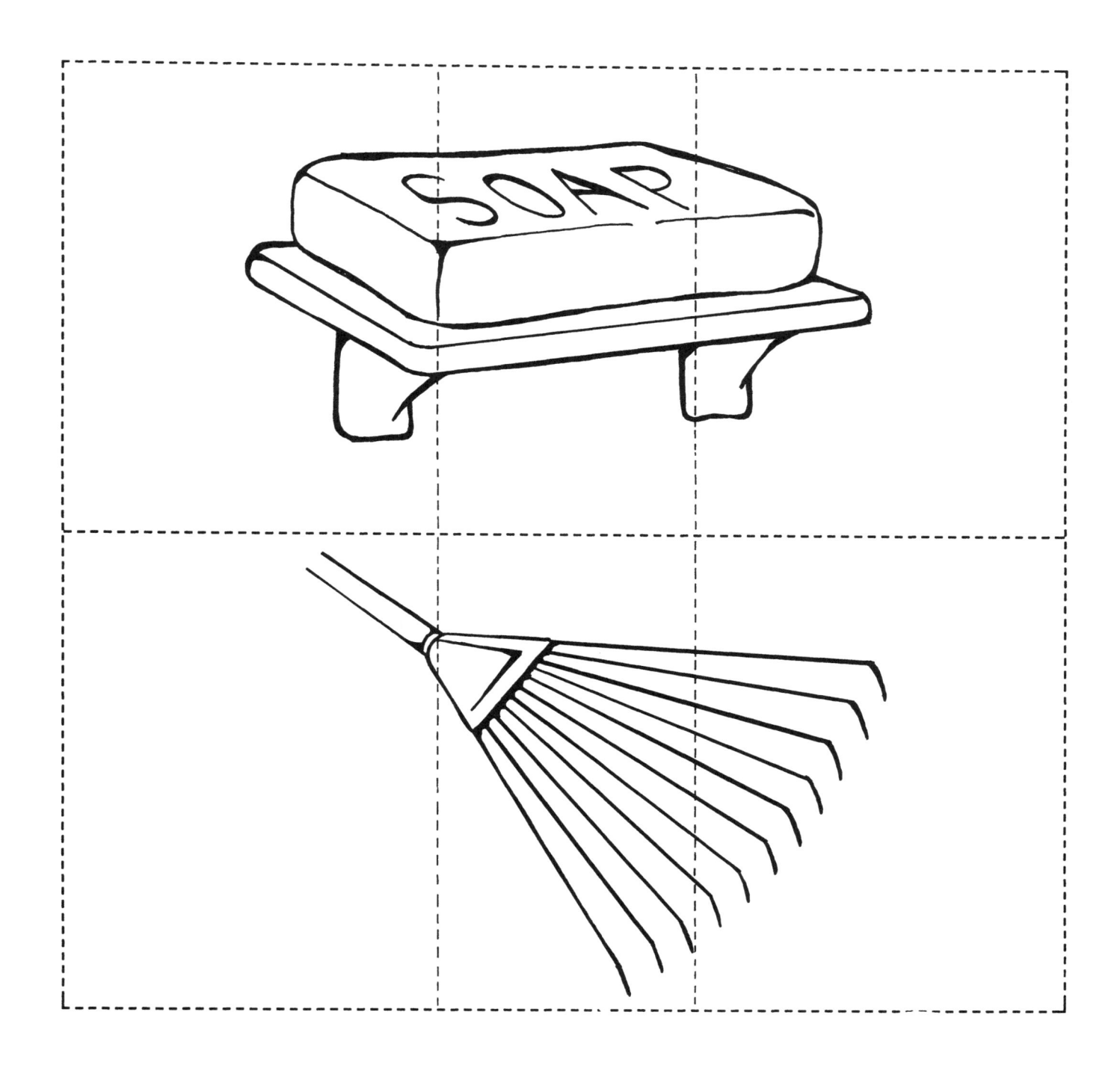

Blending   **7**   *Blending Phonemes*

Use these pictures to help the child blend phonemes.

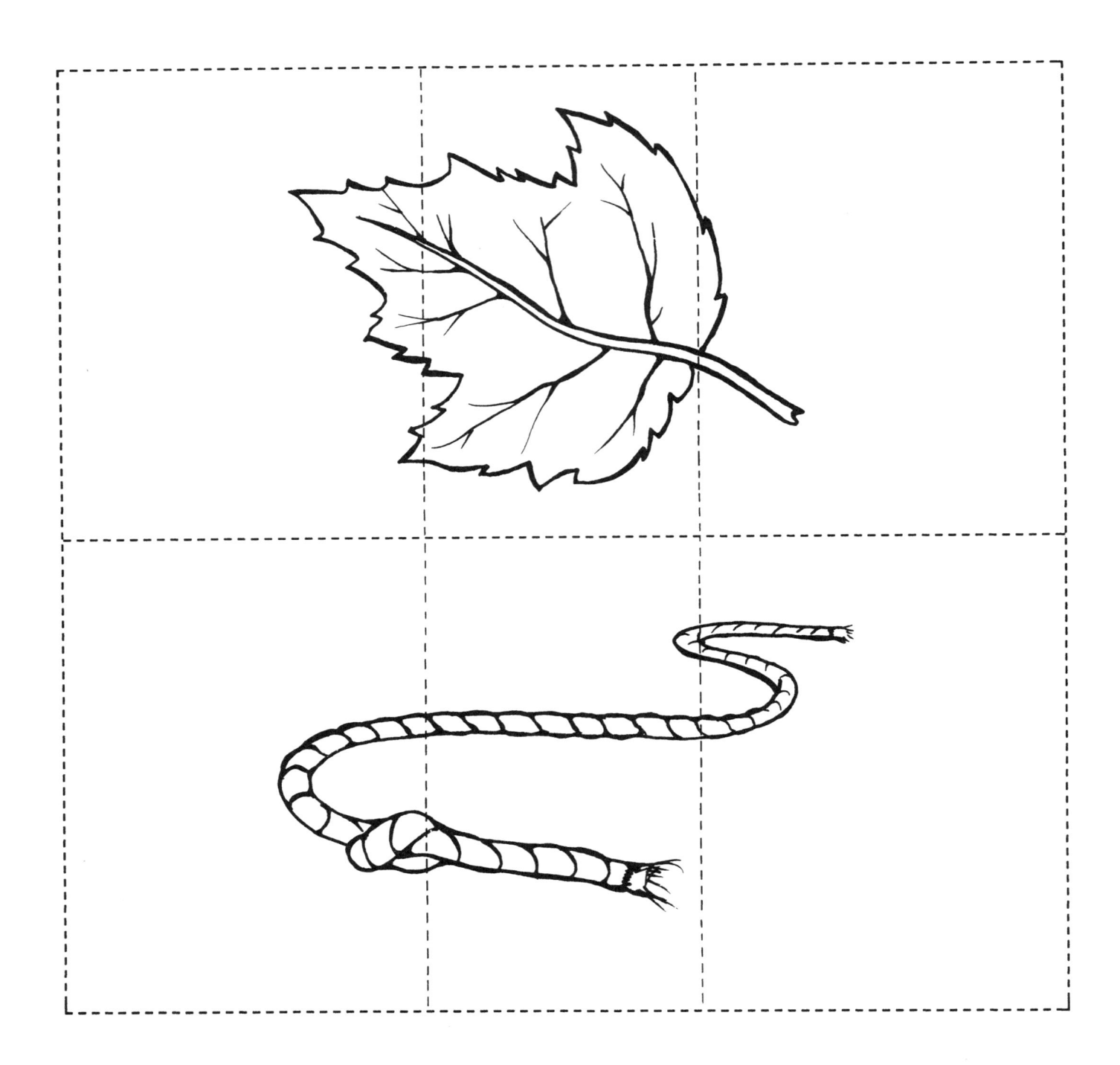

Blending

8

Blending Phonemes

Use these pictures to help the child blend phonemes.

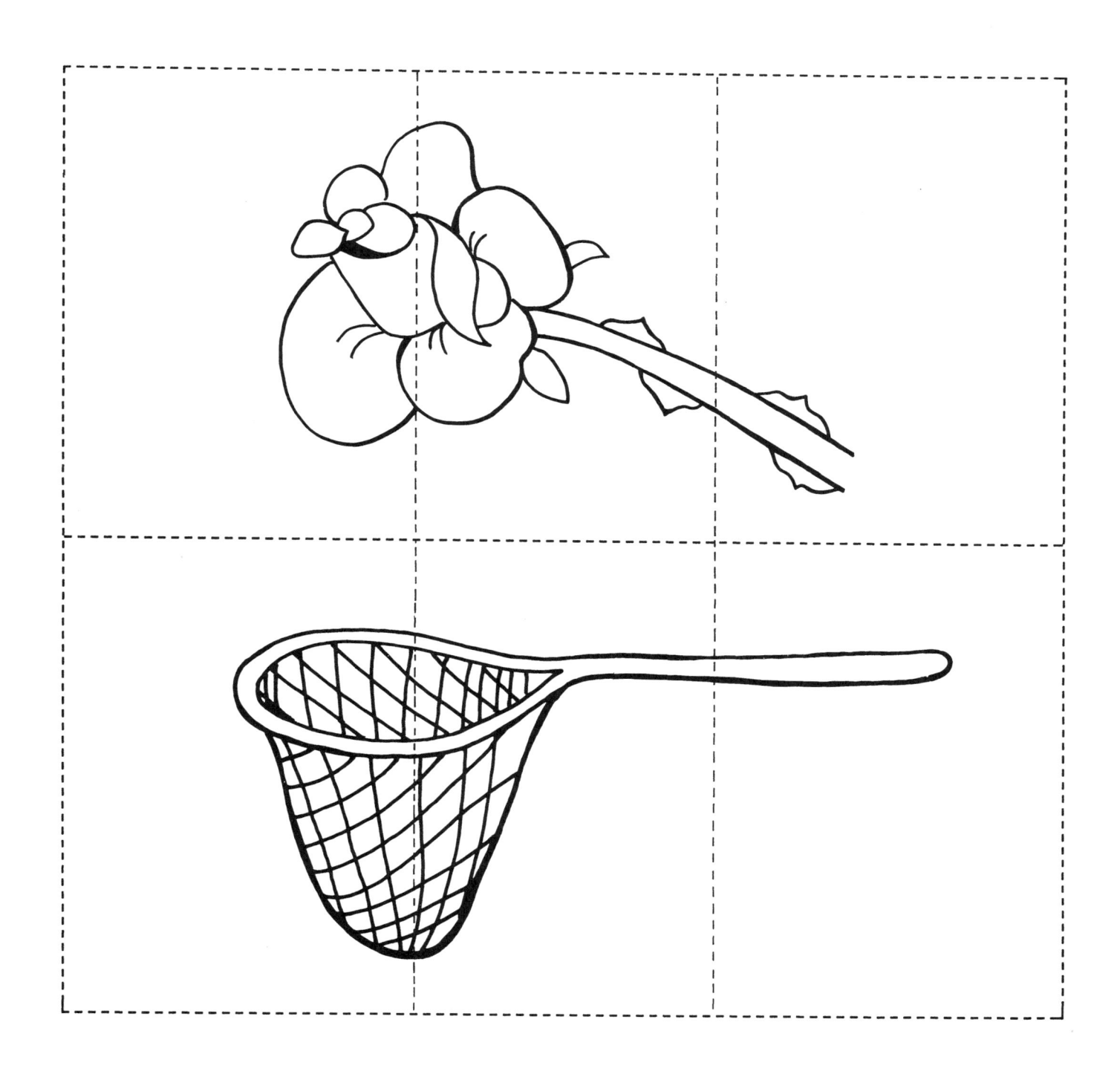

Blending 9 — *Blending Phonemes*

Read each word aloud to the child, one phoneme at a time. Then, have the child blend the phonemes together. You may want to use a hand puppet for this task. Tell the child that the puppet talks differently because he says one sound at a time. Ask the child to listen carefully to the puppet and then put the sounds together and say the word.

1. s ee
2. sh ee p
3. a pe
4. sh a ke
5. a t
6. s a fe
7. f u dge
8. sh y
9. ou t
10. ch a se
11. i t
12. ch o p
13. m i ce
14. u s
15. m ow
16. s i t
17. m y
18. j ui ce
19. s ea t
20. t ie
21. l i fe
22. sh ee t
23. s a ve
24. i f
25. r ai se
26. j ee p
27. ch ew
28. i tch
29. J a ck
30. m a ke
31. f oo t
32. j aw
33. ch ee k
34. ou ch
35. l ea ve
36. j o ke
37. n u t
38. j e t
39. f igh t
40. r a ce

Sounds Abound

Syllable/Phoneme Segmentation Pretest   *Evaluation*

This pretest uses the deletion format. Using this format, ask the child to say the word that remains after deleting the first syllable or phoneme.

There are three training items. Correct answers should only be given on the training items.

Training Items

1. sailboat
2. railroad
3. sometime

Test Items

Syllables

1. football
2. hairbrush
3. sandwich
4. motel
5. baby

Phonemes

1. fat
2. sit
3. chin
4. jar
5. meat

6. ball
7. tie
8. snow
9. flip
10. pro

Sounds Abound   175   Copyright © 1993 LinguiSystems, Inc.

Syllable/Phoneme Segmentation Posttest

Evaluation

This posttest uses the deletion format. Using this format, ask the child to say the word that remains after deleting the first syllable or phoneme.

There are three training items. Correct answers should only be given on the training items.

Training Items

1. mushroom
2. playground
3. horseshoe

Test Items

Syllables

1. popcorn
2. coughdrop
3. helpful
4. fancy
5. person

Phonemes

1. sat
2. fear
3. shin
4. chair
5. mice

6. band
7. told
8. snail
9. thread
10. prime

Sounds Abound

Syllable/Phoneme Blending Pretest *Evaluation*

Read each word aloud to the child, one segment (syllable or phoneme) at a time. Then, have the child blend the segments together. There are three training items. Correct answers should only be given on the training items.

You may want to use a hand puppet for this task. Tell the child that the puppet talks differently because he says only part of a word at a time. Ask the child to listen carefully to the puppet and then say the words the right way.

Training Items

1. doghouse
2. needle
3. captain

Test Items

Syllables

1. birthday
2. sunshine
3. brother
4. crocodile
5. December

Phonemes

1. s ay
2. n o
3. s a ck
4. l ea f
5. m ou se
6. r i ce
7. sh i p
8. l i ke
9. t o p

Sounds Abound

Syllable/Phoneme Blending Posttest *Evaluation*

Read each word aloud to the child, one segment (syllable or phoneme) at a time. Then, have the child blend the segments together. There are three training items. Correct answers should only be given on the training items.

You may want to use a hand puppet for this task. Tell the child that the puppet talks differently because he says only part of a word at a time. Ask the child to listen carefully to the puppet and then say the words the right way.

Training Items

1. outside
2. motor
3. hammer

Test Items

Syllables

1. lipstick
2. airplane
3. sister
4. people
5. uniform
6. parachute

Phonemes

1. sh ow
2. m e
3. f a t
4. s i ze
5. J oe
6. m o p
7. s i ck
8. l i p
9. t a ck

Putting Sounds Together with Letters

The awareness of the sounds of language is an important component of learning to read an alphabetic language. However, children need more than phonological awareness to learn to read. They must also understand how the alphabet is used to represent the phonemes. In other words, children must grasp the connection between the phonemes in words and the letters that represent these phonemes. For many children, particularly those at risk for reading problems, this connection is best learned through systematic and explicit instruction in a code emphasis or alphabetic approach.

This section introduces children to how the alphabet represents sounds. This is illustrated by using a subset of letters and sounds. A more extensive alphabetic program will be necessary for most children to gain a full appreciation of how the alphabet works.

Letters and Sounds

In this section, children will learn the relationship between letters and sounds and how letters are used to make words.

First, make copies of the pages in this section. Cut out the letter squares on page 181 to use with the other activity sheets. For each activity, you'll put the cut-out letter squares on top of the corresponding letter squares on the activity sheets.

Tell the children that the letters above the line represent sounds at the end of a word. Some of them spell common words, like *at* and *in*.

Next, teach the children the sounds that correspond to each of the letters below the line. Then, as you say the sound of one of the letters, move the letter to the line in front of the word ending. Blend the sound with the word ending. Repeat the activity using other letters to make more words. Finally, have the children move the letters and make the words on their own.

After the children have mastered this activity for initial consonants, use the letter squares to change the word endings and spell additional words. You may use the activity sheet on page 187 for this purpose.

Letters & Sounds 1   Name _____

Copy the letter squares below and cut them out.   Use them with pages 182-187.

s	f	m	p
r	n	t	a
e	i	o	u

Sounds Abound

Letters & Sounds 2

Name _____

Use this page to help you spell words.

[ ]	[a]	[t]
___	___	___

| [s] | [f] | [m] |

| [p] | [r] |

Letters & Sounds 3

Name _____

Use this page to help you spell words.

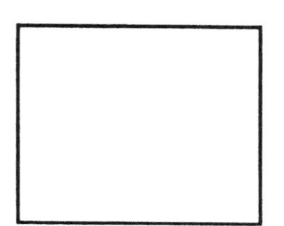

	u	n

| s | f | r | n |

Sounds Abound 183 Copyright © 1993 LinguiSystems, Inc.

Letters & Sounds 4

Name _____

Use this page to help you spell words.

| | i | n |

| s | f | p | t |

Letters & Sounds 5

Name _____

Use this page to help you spell words.

| | e | t |

| s | m | p | n |

Letters & Sounds 6

Name _____

Use this page to help you spell words.

	o	p
___	___	___

| m | p | t |

Sounds Abound 186 Copyright © 1993 LinguiSystems, Inc.

Letters & Sounds 7   Name _____

Use this page with the letters from page 181 to help you spell more words

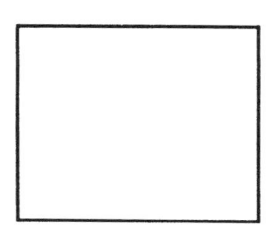

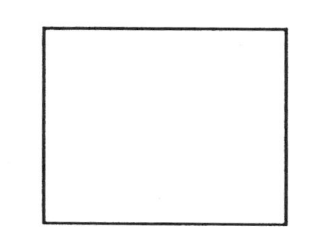

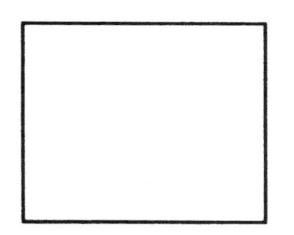

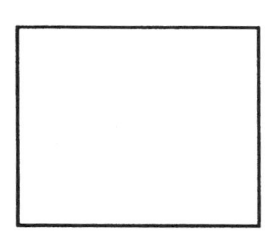

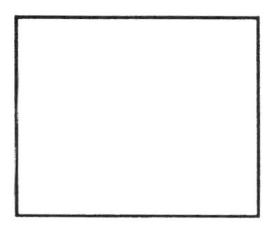

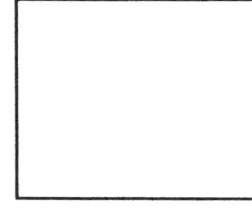

References

Aaron, P., and Joshi, M. (1992). *Reading Problems: Consultation and Remediation.* New York: The Guilford Press.

Adams, M. (1990). *Beginning To Read: Thinking and Learning about Print.* Cambridge, MA: MIT Press.

Alexander, A.; Anderson, H.; Heilman, P.; Voeller, K.; and Torgesen, J. (1991). "Phonological Awareness Training and Remediation of Analytic Decoding Deficits in a Group of Severe Dyslexics." *Annals of Dyslexia,* 41, 193-206.

Ball, E., and Blachman, B. (1988). "Phoneme Segmentation Training: Effect on Reading Readiness." *Annals of Dyslexia,* 38, 208-225.

Blachman, B. (1984). "Relationship of Rapid Naming Ability and Language Analysis Skill to Kindergarten and First-Grade Reading Achievement." *Journal of Educational Psychology,* 76, 610-622.

Bradley, L., and Bryant, P. (1983). "Categorizing Sounds and Learning to Read: A Causal Connection." *Nature,* 30, 419-421.

Bradley, L., and Bryant, P. (1985). "Rhyme and Reason in Reading and Spelling." *International Academy for Research in Learning Disabilities Monograph Series,* No. 1. Ann Arbor, MI: University of Michigan Press.

Bryant, P.; Bradley, L.; Maclean, M.; and Crossland, J. (1989). "Nursery Rhymes, Phonological Skills and Reading." *Journal of Child Language,* 16, 407-428.

Byrne, B., and Fielding-Barnsley. (1989). "Phonemic Awareness and Letter Knowledge in the Child's Acquisition of the Alphabetic Principle." *Journal of Educational Psychology,* 81, 313-321.

Catts, H. (1991a). "Early Identification of Reading Disabilities." *Topics in Language Disorders,* 12, 1-16.

Catts, H. (1991b). "Facilitating Phonological Awareness: Role of Speech-Language Pathologists." *Language, Speech, and Hearing Services in Schools,* 22, 196-203.

Cunningham, A. (1990). "Explicit vs. Implicit Instruction in Phonological Awareness." *Journal of Experimental Child Psychology.* 50, 429-444.

Fink, B., and Doyle, J. (1990). "The Public School Speech and Language Pathologist." A miniseminar presented at the annual convention of the Florida Speech-Language-Hearing Association, Miami, FL.

Fox, B., and Routh, D. (1983). "Reading Disability, Phonemic Analysis, and Dysphonetic Spelling: A Follow-Up Study." *Journal of Clinical Child Psychology,* 12, 28-32.

Goswami, U. (1990). "Phonological Priming and Orthographic Analogies in Reading." *Journal of Experimental Child Psychology*, 49, 323-340.

Kamhi, A., and Catts, H. (1989). *Reading Disabilities: A Developmental Language Perspective*. Boston, MA: Allyn and Bacon.

Lewkowicz, N. (1980). "Phonemic Awareness Training: What to Teach and How to Teach It." *Journal of Educational Psychology*, 72, 686-700.

Liberman, I.; Shankweiler, D.; Fischer, F.; and Carter, B. (1974). "Explicit Syllable and Phoneme Segmentation in Young Children." *Journal of Experimental Child Psychology*, 18, 159-173.

Lindamood, C., and Lindamood, P. (1979). *Lindamood Auditory Conceptualization Test*. Allen, TX: DLM/Teaching Resources.

Lindamood, C., and Lindamood, P. (1969). *Auditory Discrimination in Depth*. Boston, MA: Teaching Resources.

Magnusson, E., and Naucler, K. (1990). "Reading and Spelling in Language-Disordered Children– Linguistic and Metalinguistic Prerequisites: Report on a Longitudinal Study." *Clinical Linguistics and Phonetics*, 4, 49-61.

Morais, J.; Cary, L.; Alegria, J.; and Bertelson, P. (1979). "Does Awareness of Phonemes Arise Spontaneously?" *Cognition*, 7, 323-314.

Reid, C.; Zhang, Y.; Nie, H.; and Ding, B. (1986). "The Ability to Manipulate Speech Sounds Depends on Knowing Alphabetic Writing." *Cognition*, 24, 31-44.

Rosner, J., and Simon, D. (1971). "The Auditory Analysis Test: An Initial Report." *Journal of Learning Disabilities*, 4, 384-392.

Sawyer, D. (1987). *Test of Awareness of Language Segments*. Austin, TX: Pro-Ed.

Snowling, M. (1987). *Dyslexia: A Cognitive Developmental Perspective*. New York: Basil Blackwell.

Stanovich, K. (1988). "The Right and the Wrong Places to Look for the Cognitive Locus of Reading Disability." *Annals of Dyslexia*, 38, 154-180.

Stanovich, K. (1988). *Children's Reading and the Development of Phonological Awareness*. Detroit: Wayne State University Press.

Stanovich, K.; Cunningham, A.; and Cramer, B. (1984). "Assessing Phonological Awareness in Kindergarten Children: Issues of Task Comparability." *Journal of Experimental Child Psychology*, 38, 175-190.

Torgesen, J., and Bryant, B. (1993a). *Screening Test of Phonological Awareness*. Austin, TX: Pro-Ed.

Torgesen, J., and Bryant, B. (1993b). *Phonological Awareness Training for Reading*. Austin, TX: Pro-ED.

Torgesen, J.; Morgan, S.; and Davis, C. (1992). "Effects of Two Types of Phonological Awareness Training on Word Learning in Kindergarten Children." *Journal of Educational Psychology*, 84, 364-370.

Treiman, R. (1986). "The Division Between Onsets and Rimes in English Syllables." *Journal of Memory and Language*, 25, 476-491.

Tummer, W., and Nesdale, A. (1985). "Phoneme Segmentation Skill and Beginning Reading." *Journal of Educational Psychology*, 77, 417-427.

Van Kleeck, A., and Schuele, C. (1987). "Precursors to Literacy: Normal Development." *Topics in Language Disorders*, 7, 13-31.

Vellutino, F., and Scanlon, D. (1991). "The Preeminence of Phonologically Based Skills in Learning to Read." In S. Brady and D. Shankweiler (Eds.). *Phonological Processes in Literacy*. Hillsdale, NJ: Lawrence Erlbaum Associates.

Wagner, R., and Torgesen, J. (1987). "The Nature of Phonological Processing and Its Causal Role in the Acquisition of Reading Skills." *Psychological Bulletin*, 101, 192-212.

Williams, J. (1980). "Teaching Decoding with an Emphasis on Phoneme Analysis and Phoneme Blending." *Journal of Educational Psychology*, 72, 1-15.

Williams, J. (1979). "The ABD's of Reading: A Program for the Learning Disabled." In L. Resnick and P. Weaver (Eds.), *Theory and Practice of Early Reading*, 3 (pp. 179-195). Hillsdale, NJ: Lawrence Erlbaum.

Wise, B.; Olson, R.; and Treiman, R. (1990). "Subsyllabic Units in Computerized Reading Instruction: Onset-Rime vs. Postvowel Segmentation." *Journal of Experimental Child Psychology*, 49, 1-19.

Yopp, H. (1988). *The Validity and Reliability of Phonemic Awareness Tests*. Reading Research Quarterly, 23, 159-177.

Yopp, H. (1992). *Developing Phonological Awareness in Young Children*. The Reading Teacher, 45, 696-703.